SAILBOAT CHARTERING

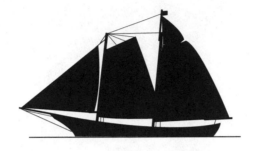

SAILBOAT CHARTERING
THE COMPLETE GUIDE AND INTERNATIONAL DIRECTORY

by
Melvin H. Ross
and
James P. Duffy

A Voyager Book

The Globe Pequot Press

Old Saybrook, Connecticut

Photo credits: p. 1: Whitsunday Rent A Yacht; p. 35: John Perkins photograph courtesy of The Moorings; p. 105: © Helge Baardseth, courtesy of Lofoten Charter Boats, Norway. All others by Melvin Ross unless otherwise noted.

Library of Congress Cataloging-in-Publication Data

Ross, Melvin H.
   Sailboat chartering : the complete guide and international
directory / by Melvin H. Ross & James P. Duffy. — 1st ed.
   p.   cm.
"A Voyager book."
ISBN 1-56440-137-5
   1. Sailboats—Chartering. 2. Sailboats—Chartering—Directories.
I. Duffy, James P., 1941- . II. Title.
GV811.R587 1993
797.1'24—dc20   92-36028
                              CIP

Manufactured in the United States of America
First Edition/First Printing

For Eddie Jacobs and Bob Reibel. To Eddie, the best of shipmates, whose sailing ability, good humor, and good fellowship have turned many a cruise into a treasure chest of memories. And to Bob, for introducing me to sailing so many years ago. For these gifts I thank them both. For their friendship I can't thank them enough.

MHR

CONTENTS

Part Three: Worldwide Directory of Charter Operators

Map of Sailing Areas

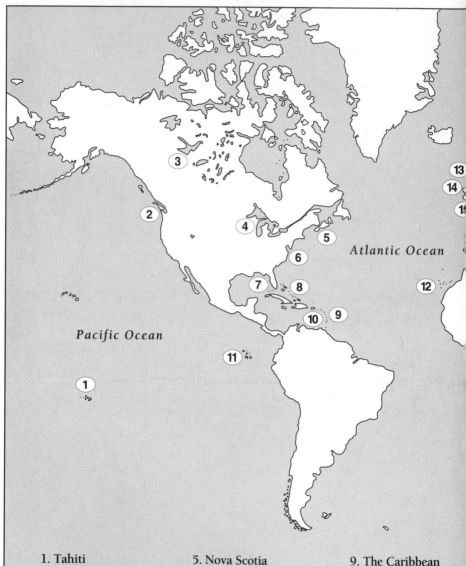

Atlantic Ocean

Pacific Ocean

1. Tahiti
2. San Juan Islands
3. Great Slave Lake
4. Great Lakes

5. Nova Scotia
6. U.S. East Coast
7. Florida Keys
8. The Bahamas

9. The Caribbean
10. Venezuela
11. Galapagos Islands
12. Canary Islands

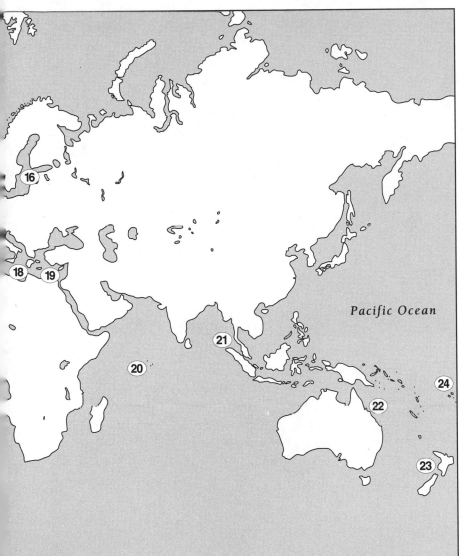

Pacific Ocean

13. Scotland
14. Ireland
15. Norfolk Broads
16. Finland

17. Corsica and Sardinia
18. Greece
19. Turkey
20. Seychelle Islands

21. Thailand
22. Whitsunday Islands
23. New Zealand
24. Fiji Islands

Chartering for the Fun of It

Sailing is addictive. The more we sail the more we want to sail. We may start out with a small boat, but gradually get bigger and bigger craft as our sailing expands from a couple of hours at a time to day-sailing to weekend cruises. Meanwhile, we read the classic books of the Hiscocks, the Pardeys, Joshua Slocum, Tristan Jones, Hal Roth, and others, and we dream of sailing to faraway places.

Some of our dreams are heroic, such as battling Cape Horn and the Roaring Forties. Other visions may be more modest: cruising Chesapeake Bay or the islands of Maine or the San Juan Islands. In any case, when the snow is piling up outside, it's hard not to think about lying on a white-sand beach with our perfect yacht gently rising and falling to the anchor in crystal-clear water.

Aside from the pleasures of sailing and seeing areas we have read about, cruising offers another major benefit: meeting people with cultural backgrounds that are different from our own and experiencing those cultures firsthand. There is no better way to do this than from a small boat, which provides access to areas that cannot be reached in any other way and that, in many cases, have not been inundated with tourists. As a result, the welcome you receive tends to be genuine and much friendlier than in the hot tourist spots, where selling souvenirs is often the primary concern of the locals. Furthermore, arriving in a small boat rather than in a cruise ship allows you to meet people on a more informal level, learn more about their everyday lives, and even establish lasting friendships. This is the case not only in foreign countries, but in your own country as well. The small-boat sailor is more often treated as a guest rather than as just another tourist.

But let's face it: Despite the many benefits of cruising, few of us can chuck the obligations of job, home, family, and friends for

Fun for all ages on a Caribbean charter (*John Perkins photo courtesy of The Moorings*)

the extended periods required to cruise the world. Generally, this would mean taking off for anywhere from one to three years. But this doesn't mean we can't go cruising in many of the exotic, exciting areas we read about. The answer is chartering.

Why Charter?

Let's look at the advantages of chartering over trying to cruise in our own boat.

Time Flexibility

One of the principal restraints on cruising is time. Let's say you want to cruise in Hawaii for two weeks. By the time you sail from California to Hawaii in your own boat (assuming your boat, crew, and sailing experience are adequate to get you there in the first place), it's time to return home—with no time for cruising Hawaii. Most of us just don't have the time to sail to cruising grounds and to then spend more time traveling the area. But chartering gives you the flexibility to adapt the time to your needs. If you suddenly find you have five days to yourself—not enough time to go to one of the more distant destinations—you might still fly down to the Florida Keys for five wonderful days of cruising. You can charter for five days, one week, two weeks, or whatever your needs dictate. Some charterers even let you pick up the boat at one location and drop it off at another. Thus, you don't have to retrace your steps and you can cover a greater area in a relatively short time.

Choice of Boat

You may own a great twenty-foot sloop, fine for day-sailing or overnighters but not for two weeks of living aboard. Or you may own a hot racer, terrific for rounding the race course—but with no bunks, no head, no galley, it's "no way" for cruising. You need a boat that is safe to sail in the area you will visit, suitable for the number of crew, and with the equipment (depth finder, reliable motor, galley, dinghy, etc.) necessary for safety, comfort, and enjoyment. Sure, you can buy such a boat and have it available at all times. But why buy more boat than you need for your normal type of sailing? It would mean greater initial expenditure and greater upkeep all year round. Chartering allows you to get the type of boat you need just when you need it.

The vast majority of sailors use their own boats for relatively short periods of sailing. They don't normally have boats large enough or equipped adequately for cruising. So it makes sense for sailors to rent or charter a boat for the periods they do want to cruise. On one occasion, you might enjoy a sail in the Ionian Islands with two or three friends on a twenty-eight-footer. Next time out you may be sailing the Windward Islands with six aboard—and you can then simply charter a different boat.

Fitting Your Experience to the Charter

Most sailors learn early on to respect the sea. No matter how good a sailor you are, you're in a hostile environment more powerful than you could ever hope to be. So we learn about sailing, the wind, the waves, the weather. For some people, however, the feeling that they don't know enough about sailing results in limiting their experiences. They're afraid their skills and knowledge are inadequate for cruising. But there is a charter available for every level of skill, from the "old salt" with top-notch boat handling and navigation skills to the novice sailor. We will cover this subject in detail in the next chapter. For now, just be assured that there is a charter suitable for you, no matter how much or how little skill you have as a sailor.

Crew Members

The crew is another factor. Cruising with family or friends is enjoyable, but what if you are alone? Chartering provides an answer. Many charterers will arrange to make you part of a compatible crew, taking into account your sailing experience, type of people you like to associate with, age, and so on. Similarly, let's say two of you would like to go cruising, but only one of you knows how to sail. Chartering can help by joining you up with another short-handed crew or by providing a crewed bareboat charter (described in the next chapter).

Fun

The biggest reason for chartering is that it's fun. Every charter results in long-lasting memories that make you smile, chuckle, or just feel good whenever they come to mind. You will visit places that will enchant you with their beauty, their history, their people, their customs, and their food. Along the way you are sure to make long-lasting friendships with crew from other boats or people you meet in the local area.

Chartering gives you the opportunity to combine your love of sailing with the adventure of seeing new places and meeting new people. No words can adequately describe the sun setting as you sit in your cockpit in a lovely anchorage. Or the sun rising as the mist slowly burns off the water and you gaze at the little jewel of an island across the bay. Or the dolphins smiling up at you as they criss-cross your bow.

Each charter offers new experiences, even if you're sailing in an area you've sailed before. There is always something new, something unique to this cruise. In addition, there is a feeling of accomplishment. You've seen an area, you've navigated successfully, and you've done it in a sailboat. You've worked with nature—the wind and the waves—and you've gotten the elements to help you go where you wanted.

Chartering offers the fun and thrills of cruising without having to choose a different life-style. (It's one of the few times in life when you can have your cake and eat it too.) The purpose of this book is to help guide you through the chartering process. Much like sailing itself, you'll find that the more you charter, the more you want to charter. So, don't just sit there in your armchair and daydream. Get out there and do it. Happy sailing!

Part One:
How to Charter a Sailboat

A Charter for Every Sailor

No matter what your level of sailing experience, there is a charter for you. In fact, different types of charters may be appropriate at different times. Regardless of the type of charter you choose, you will have the opportunity to become familiar with a boat that is new to you.

The Charter Boat

Learning a new boat—its design, handling characteristics, and equipment—can be one of the most interesting aspects of chartering. The boats we charter tend to be larger than those we normally sail. Don't let this scare you off. Most of us learned to sail on small boats, and, believe it or not, this has probably made us better sailors. Things happen fast in a small boat: You heel over in a relatively light breeze, you come about fast, you change heading at the least pressure on the tiller. With a larger boat things tend to happen at a much slower pace: It takes more wind to heel over, it takes longer to tack, the heavier boat needs somewhat more time to respond. Particularly if you have been sailing a centerboard/daggerboard/drop-keel boat, you will feel the greater stability as you sail a chartered keel boat with a fair amount of displacement. This will affect the way you anchor or come into a quay or dock because a heavy boat has more carry, or way, than a lighter one. So you'll need a little practice with the boat once you get out on the open water—really the same thing you would do when handling any boat you were unfamiliar with.

Nearly every charter boat of any size is equipped with a reliable inboard diesel motor of sufficient power to get you where you want to go. Many of us are accustomed to outboards hanging off the transom; once you get used to the diesel, you'll find a great

72-foot sloop off the British Virgin Islands *(Jim Raycroft photo courtesy of The Moorings)*

deal of security in its relative dependability, power, and ease of operation. When you are in an unfamiliar area coming into a bay or anchorage that has coral or rocks, it's great to have the precise control of a reliable motor without the worry of short-tacking or wind shifts. It's also nice to know that if the wind dies, or if the weather turns foul and you don't feel like sailing, you have a motor that can take you good distances in good time.

If you normally sail a small boat, you may be accustomed to hoisting the main halyard by hand and trimming the jib sheets without mechanical aid. On a larger boat you will have winches that take most of the strain, sometimes two-speed and often self-tailing, and frequently a mechanical or even electrical windlass to help raise the anchor. A larger boat will also have a head, a galley, and usually at least one shower.

Your boat will normally have a knotmeter and a depth finder. Keeping track of compass heading, speed, and water depth, plus a visual scan of the surroundings, will generally allow you to pinpoint your location on your chart. (It's surprising, however, how easy it is to mistake one bay for another on a coastline with multiple bays and indentations.) In most instances you will not need advanced navigational know-how and will not have to use celestial or electronic navigation. But you will need piloting skills, including good skills in coastal navigation—setting and following a compass course, keeping track of your location, reading a chart. You will rarely be out in open, featureless water, but rather will be following a shoreline or line-of-sight string of islands. Piloting is important to help you get where you want to go and to keep you out of harm's way (such as underwater reefs at shallow depths).

You will be briefed by the charterer about the systems on your boat—where things are, and how to operate the engine, radio, depth finder, head, and other equipment. You will not be turned loose on a boat that is strange to you. After all, the charterer wants to be assured you know how to handle the boat and its equipment.

Types of Charters

There are three basic types of charters, plus a variation on the theme. Each offers different opportunities and may require different levels of skill or experience, although the same person may enjoy each type of charter depending upon the situation and the crew. The basic types are bareboat charters, crewed bareboat charters, and flotilla charters. The variation is offered by sailing schools, which provide both instruction and cruises.

Bareboat Charters

Bareboat chartering gives you the greatest degree of freedom—and the greatest degree of responsibility. You will pick up your boat from the charterer at a specific time, take charge of it, and return it at a specific time. It's up to you where you sail (within the confines of the chartering area), where you anchor, when you leave an area, and when you eat, swim, sleep, or whatever. She's your boat and your responsibility.

When you contact a chartering company, you will be sent information on the types of boats available, accommodations provided on the boats, and the geographic area the charters encompass. You will also get details on prices at high and low season; the cost varies with the desirability of the time of year in that part of the world. You'll usually be expected to provide a refundable deposit. The cost of the boat is usually divided among the crewmembers, so with a crew of five it will cost each of you one-fifth of the total amount. The charterer will explain what experience you need in order to obtain a bareboat charter and will usually ask you to fill out a questionnaire documenting your sailing background. Once you contract with a charterer, you will usually receive a set of charts and/or a chartering guide to the area. If it's a foreign country, the charterer may provide information on local customs, the monetary system, and required inoculations, plus a small glossary of terms in the local language. Make sure you obtain the above information for all areas you plan to sail, even if the charterer doesn't provide it.

It's best to contract early with the charter company in order to get the boat you want at the time you want. Also, getting all the information well in advance prolongs your enjoyment. You will have time to plan your itinerary and revise it, and to read up on the area to determine where you want to go. Be realistic within the time you have for cruising. Keep in mind that you're in a sailboat—not a jetliner—and don't expect to cover more distance than is reasonable. You are probably sailing in an area new and strange to you. With this thought in mind, charter companies usually forbid night sailing. (It's one way they help protect their investment in boats usually worth between $100,000 and $300,000.) It can be difficult to determine how much time you will want to spend in any particular spot until you get there, so give yourself some flexibility and alternatives. A rainy day may make exploring a town or village more enticing than a wet sail. An unusual wind shift may make a beam reach to another island more appealing than a long beat into the wind. A great reef can make another day of snorkeling a must. So plan your route—but keep in mind that some parts of it are bound to change.

Your crew will also influence your plans. If you have a crew of experienced sailors, you may plan somewhat longer sails. Non-sailors, especially at the start of the trip, may need a little more time to get adjusted to their new environment and may also want more time ashore. It is a good idea to reach an agreement on the itinerary, at least in general, before the start of the trip.

You might have a full crew of expert sailors, but you could also have a short-handed crew, or a crew that combines non-sailors, novice sailors, and experts. In any case, carefully determine the crew's compatibility. Different types of personalities may conflict, especially in a small living space. And even a forty-four-foot sailboat affords little real privacy. The chances are that if people get along together ashore, they will get along on a boat. Don't force two conflicting personalities into a cruise because you would like to be with both of them. Chances are it will ruin everyone's trip.

If your crew is composed of experienced sailors and a sufficient number to handle the boat, you're ready to plan the trip. Otherwise, take a look at your crew members, and determine how many you can count on to know how to sail, how many can help after you provide some training, and how many will simply be passengers. Then decide if this mix is adequate to handle the boat. In most instances it is. If you're going with a raw crew, it's a good idea to take them out as many times as you can on your own boat before leaving for the charter in order to familiarize them with boating. Once on the charter boat, explain things to the novices—how the head works, what jobs you want them to do, and so forth. Explain the names of things to non-sailors. Don't take it for granted that the names are self-explanatory; they weren't when *you* were learning.

Keep one critical factor in mind in organizing a crew: there is only one captain. Even with an experienced crew, there should be one agreed-upon leader. The decision to shorten sail or to tack should not be a committee decision. This philosophy has to be understood before the trip begins. That doesn't mean the crew has no input—but in nautical matters, the captain's orders are the ones that count, for everyone's safety.

Make travel arrangements well in advance. Charter companies often have an arrangement with an airline that will give you a discount. The charterer will usually make arrangements to pick you up at your charter destination's airport and to return you to the airport after your cruise, but if they don't, be sure to arrange ground transportation. Depending upon the location and the time of your arrival, you may go directly to your boat or stay overnight at facilities owned or arranged for by the charterer.

The charterer will give a thorough briefing on the cruising area—desirable places to go, water hazards, etc.—while going over the charts with you. You will also be briefed on how to work the radio, the head, the roller furling and windlass, the motor, the stove, and all other equipment on your boat. Most charterers will ensure radio contact with you throughout the cruising area in case of emergency. Your boat will come with a dinghy, allowing you to anchor offshore and still be able to go shoreside. The dinghy, usually powered by an outboard motor (but with auxiliary oars), also lets you explore areas too shallow or narrow to get your boat safely through.

Your charterer may offer you options for provisioning. In some areas you must rely on the charter company because there is no other way to secure food. Usually you are given options ranging from full provisioning (sometimes with a choice of menus) to partial provisioning (in which you supplement the food provided by the charterer) to independent provisioning (in which you do the provisioning yourself). Full provisioning is the least hassle for yourself: everything is provided (except liquor). The menu, however, may include items that you or others on the crew don't like. It's also the most expensive way of provisioning. Partial provisioning usually provides the basics (such as bread, bottled water, and food for several meals). If you are in an area where you can easily shop, it can be a lot of fun buying your own food and supplies. You get to see local foods, see the stores, talk to shopkeepers and get their advice (usually good), and select foods that appeal to you and your crew, and in the long run, you will usually save a little money while experiencing some of the local flavor (in more ways than one).

Cruising the Whitsunday Islands, Australia (Whitsunday Rent a Yacht)

In planning your itinerary, figure out the approximate number of meals you will need to prepare on board. Keep in mind your crew and the cruising grounds. You might want to eat dinners ashore and prepare the simpler meals of breakfast and lunch aboard ship, except when planning an anchorage without shoreside eating facilities. When cruising abroad, dinners can be cheap by U.S. standards—$3.00 including beverage and tip is not unusual in places like the Greek Islands, Turkey, and Thailand. Eating out can be very interesting: new foods, new methods of preparation, and a chance to meet the locals. Unless you have a crew member who really wants to cook and you would all rather eat on the boat, consider the pleasant alternative of having dinner ashore.

The primary pleasure of bareboating is the freedom you have. You and your crew can sail and visit anywhere within the cruising area all on your own timetable. If you feel like more sailing, go for it. If you would rather spend time ashore exploring a lovely beach or an ancient ruin or a quaint village, it's up to you. For the period of the charter, this is your boat taking you where you want, when you want. It's a rare charter that doesn't end with you wishing it could continue. While the bareboat charter gives you maximum freedom, it also imposes the greatest responsibility. You, as skipper, have the ultimate responsibility for an expensive boat and, more importantly, the safety of your crew.

You don't need to be a hot racing skipper to cruise efficiently on a bareboat. You do need good boat handling, anchoring, and piloting skills, and enough crew members to safely handle the boat. In general, two knowledgeable sailors can handle a boat up to twenty-nine feet; from thirty to forty-four feet it may require three (one of whom may not be very experienced). Inexperienced sailors can contribute by raising or lowering sails, trimming sheets, helping with the anchor, launching the dinghy, cooking, and cleaning. Many landlubbers enjoy the experience of taking the wheel or tiller as you teach them to sail. It is beneficial for all crew members to have jobs to do aboard. It keeps them occupied and makes them feel they are contributing to the success of the cruise—and they are! It will soon become apparent which novice crew members want to learn more and which have the physical or mental skills for the jobs you assign them. Like much of life, the more a person contributes to the cruise, the more that person gets out of it.

The first day of a bareboat charter should be taken slowly, with only a modest distance to the first destination. This gives everyone a chance to become acquainted with the boat. While out in open water, turn on the engine to get a feel for how the boat acts under power, including reverse gear (most sailing boats tend to be sluggish in reverse). Then when you need the engine, you will have more confidence in its operation. When winds are light is a good time to show your crew (if inexperienced) how to reef the sails; don't wait until the real thing comes along. The first day is for learning the boat and easing into the cruising mode. This helps to make sure that on the last day everyone is saying, "Let's plan the next charter."

Crewed Bareboat Charters

As in basic bareboat chartering, crewed bareboats are chartered for a specific length of time. The difference is that you also pay for a crew—either skipper alone or, more likely, a full crew with both a skipper and a mate. It is the crew's responsibility to handle the boat, keep it clean and provisioned, and make sure you are happy and well fed (the mate is often an excellent cook). It's something like having your own floating hotel.

You discuss with the skipper where you would like to go, what you like to eat, what you would like to do, and when you would like to do it. You can count on the skipper being a competent sailor and also very knowledgeable about the area. As a result, you also have a built-in tour guide. The skipper will know the beautiful beaches, the reefs for the best snorkeling, the sights to see, and the restaurants ashore that are worth visiting. You are usually free to help with the sailing as much as you would like— or not at all if that is your wish. You have the independence of a bareboat charter, but someone else has the responsibility for the boat. That "someone else" is the skipper, so remember that in nautical decisions, you must defer to the skipper.

There are a variety of good reasons why you might decide on a crewed bareboat. First of all, some sailing areas offer only crewed charters. But in other locations you may not feel capable of handling the boat or of sailing the area. Or perhaps your group doesn't include enough trained crew members.

The best reason may simply be that you want to take it easy and enjoy yourself with as little physical or mental labor as possible. Many an experienced sailor has had a wonderful cruise just lying back and acting like a guest. It's a chance to feel super-pampered without any guilt.

Naturally, a crewed charter is somewhat more expensive than a bareboat since you must pay for the crew. But many people feel it is well worth the expense.

Flotilla Charters

Flotilla cruising is somewhat newer on the sailing scene, having been developed in the last eighteen years or so. It is a cross between conventional bareboating and crewed bareboats. You and your crew charter the boat and are responsible for sailing it. The difference is that you go out with a group, or "flotilla," of chartered boats, with a lead boat crewed by a professional skipper and a bosun, or engineer. You are provided in advance with charts and information on the sailing area. Usually the crews for the various boats are booked on a charter flight by the flotilla cruising compa-

A three-boat flotilla stops over in the British Virgin Islands *(Caribbean Yacht Charters, Inc.)*

ny. The cost of the charter often includes airfare plus ground transportation at the sailing destination.

The first morning of a flotilla charter is devoted to familiarizing you with your boat and its various systems—engine, galley, rigging, radio, head, and so forth. A thorough skipper's briefing covers the area to be sailed the first day. The lead boat contains spare parts, and the bosun is trained to repair virtually anything that can go wrong with your boat. Often there is also a hostess on the lead boat who briefs you on certain specifics about the ports you will be visiting: where you can buy food, where you can change money, where laundry can be done, where to mail letters, which restaurants are recommended, and so on. Some flotilla companies provide booklets with magnified views of harbor plans, phrases in the local language, and information on the local currency and sights to see.

After the first skipper's meeting, you sail off somewhat like ducklings following the mother duck—in this case a lead boat that may have a special color jib to make it easy to identify. You have your own set of detailed charts, but on this first day all you really have to do is follow the lead boat. The first day's sail is normally a short one. The skipper in the lead boat helps everyone tie up to the quay or drop anchor. When the entire fleet is together—usually ten to twelve boats—the hostess arranges for everyone to have dinner in the same restaurant. The first night becomes a get-acquainted time, and virtually every time the fleet gets together like this, it becomes a party.

On some flotilla cruises the group stays together the entire time. In most areas, however, there is a considerable amount of free sailing time. After the first day you will get another thorough briefing on the sailing area, but you may then have two or three days of free sailing. During this period you can sail off where you wish, just as you would with a bareboat. If you prefer, you can stay with the main body of the flotilla, depending on how secure you feel sailing alone and on how much you want to socialize. The entire fleet meets again at a designated time and place. When the entire fleet meets again, you will usually have dinner together in a local restaurant. Some flotilla charterers have the lead boat host an island barbecue once during the trip; you bring the firewood while the lead crew does the cooking.

The flotilla then heads out to another spot, although after the first day, flotilla sails are generally freer, requiring only that you arrive at a certain point by a certain time. Sometimes a special trip is arranged for the entire fleet to visit some unusual or interesting site and you may again have the option of independent sailing or sailing with the fleet. The degree of privacy you can enjoy on a flotilla cruise is up to you. When you feel like getting off on your own, you can; when you feel like having company, that's available, too.

The first time I (Mel) went flotilla sailing I had major misgivings. One of the wonderful things about a sailing vacation is the freedom you feel. Having chartered bareboats, I was worried that a group cruise would make me feel restricted and the sometimes pleasant feeling of isolation would disappear. These fears were soon alleviated. I found that the free sailing days gave me more than enough time to do my own thing. The camaraderie of the sailors on the other boats added tremendously to the overall enjoyment of the cruise. Sometimes during free sailing I would meet up with another of the flotilla boats, and it was like meeting an old friend. When the fleet was together, it really was like a super party. I met Eddie Jacobs, who eventually became my best friend, when he was sailing one of the other flotilla boats. We subsequently did a lot of sailing together, some flotilla and some bareboat, with more to come, I hope.

If you are somewhat insecure about your ability to cruise alone, flotilla chartering is the answer. When you are with the fleet, you have not only the lead boat to provide help or guidance but also the crews of the other boats in the flotilla. You become part of one large expanded family. At least once on each flotilla sail I've been on, I've seen someone throw out an anchor without attaching the end, resulting in a little embarrassment but in every instance a lot of help retrieving the anchor, followed by some good-natured kidding. Flotilla charters offer a good way to gain enough experience to make you ready for a bareboat charter. As a means to cruise when you don't feel entirely capable, as a way to learn to cruise, or just as a different way of chartering, flotilla charters have a lot to offer.

Sailing Schools

Professional sailing instruction can be a gateway to charter cruising. Some sailing schools offer courses—either a basic sailing course followed by a shared cruise, or a cruising course followed by a cruise. These courses are good for sailing or cruising novices, but even "old salts" tend to learn something new from instruction by trained professionals.

The courses can range from basic sailing lessons to more advanced how-to-cruise courses, where you may earn a certificate authenticating your ability to bareboat. The courses include both classroom and on-the-water training; knowledgeable, trained teachers lead you through the course, and the classes tend to be small, which assures you of individual attention. The literature from the school will usually indicate whether the instructors have Coast Guard licenses or if they have been certified by organizations such as the American Sailing Association or the Red Cross.

The courses are fairly intense, but not so intense as to forget that part of the objective is to enjoy yourself. Some schools have evening classes, but the curriculum will always include time for fun. These combination school/cruise vacations give you the opportunity to learn sailing or cruising from trained instructors whose objective is to teach you in a short period of time the right way to do it and to then provide you with the fun of an actual cruise. After the training you will go with classmates and an instructor on a cruise to practice what you've learned. The presence of an instructor assures you that you won't get into trouble, and that if you do goof you'll be shown the correct way to do it. We probably all learn more from our mistakes than from anything else.

With all the chartering options, there is a suitable one for any occasion and for any level of sailing skill. You can bareboat for the maximum freedom if your sailing ability permits it. Or take a crewed bareboat if you want to completely relax but still want the fun of a cruise (or if your crew is inexperienced). Go for the flotilla charter if you feel a little insecure or just for the fun of a new way of chartering with a built-in social life. Try the school/cruise alternative to quickly learn new sailing skills combined with a cruise. You can try these various options even if you are alone or with just one other person; some charter outfits will arrange to team you up with others of similar skill to make a charter cruise possible. No matter which option you try, you're bound to have a good time if you like sailing and like seeing new places and meeting new people. There's a lot to see out there, and no better way to see it than from a cruising boat.

How to Select
the Right Charter for You

It takes a good bit of thought to decide on the charter adventure you'd like to undertake. You need to settle on a cruising area and to select a specific charterer and type of charter—all the time taking into account the likes and dislikes, the strengths and weaknesses, of your cruising companions.

First of all, which areas are most interesting to you and your shipmates? You may want to start by listing broad areas such as the Caribbean or the Mediterranean. Then you can start the sifting process to decide which specific locales have the greatest appeal. A key to the success of the trip is selecting an area that has appeal and activities to interest all of the crew. Chances are that you know sailing friends who have already chartered. Ask them about their trips both in terms of what they liked about the cruising area and their experience with the charterer.

Think about the kind of experience you are looking for. What is it you really want to do? If you want long sails, you can do this one of two ways: seek areas that by nature require a fair amount of sailing between ports, or just select your destinations so that you get the desired amount of sailing you want (for instance, go to every other island on the way south, and on the return trip stop at the islands you missed on the way down). If one of your prime objectives is snorkeling or scuba diving, certainly you want to determine that there are good coral reefs in an area. If fishing is one of your kicks, find out what type of fishing is done in the area. If you want to go swimming off pristine white sand beaches, then you don't want an area where few if any beaches exist. So, set your priorities.

What type of shoreside activities are you looking for? Do you want to visit quaint villages with a foreign flavor? Would you occasionally want to find a nightclub? Are towns with good shop-

Serpentine Cove in majestic Harriman Fjord, Alaska (*Alaskan Wilderness Sailing Safaris*)

ping important to you? Do you want to explore ancient ruins or take side trips to famous sites? Another important question: do you want to do most of the cooking aboard ship or do you want to be able to eat in restaurants or tavernas most evenings? The answers to these questions will help define which areas on your list will be best for this particular trip.

The time of year and the climate for that time of year will be a factor in your decision. Cruising the islands of Maine may be terrific in July or August but not in December or January. Climate is certainly a consideration if your chartering vacation must be done at a specific time of year and you're unable to schedule it for when the climate is best in a particular location. Most charterers have their seasons scheduled according to local climate conditions, but this is not always the case, so be sure to ask. Unless you suffer from masochistic tendencies, you undoubtedly prefer sailing without fog, and in sunshine rather than rain (although some of my English buddies have told me, "If we don't sail in the rain, we don't sail."). Most of us are not that hardy though.

Another factor is cost. Except where airfare is part of the total package, you have to consider the cost of getting to and from the chartering area as part of your total cost. The time of year will also have an impact on cost. Most chartering areas have "high" and "low" seasons, corresponding to the most desirable times of chartering or when the greatest demand occurs. Caribbean charters, for example, usually cost more during winter. The difference in cost may be sufficient for you to consider going at another time of year.

Don't forget the political environment of an area. While the physical desirability of cruising an area seldom changes, the political situation may. Keep abreast of current events if you're planning a foreign charter. If the situation seems "hairy," it might make sense to think of another sailing area and to reconsider your original choice when things have calmed down. You don't want to find out at the last minute that your charter is canceled due to war, or that your chances of being treated hospitably are minimal due to current political unrest.

Once you've narrowed your choice of cruising area down to a workable number of locations, think in terms of the sailing area and the amount of cruising experience required to sail there if you intend to bareboat. Also consider whether a flotilla charter or crewed bareboat would be better for you, and whether they are available in the area. (See the previous chapter for full descriptions of bareboat, crewed, and flotilla charters.) The makeup of your crew will influence this decision, based on the number of people in your cruising party, the quality of their sailing skills, and the size of boat needed. With a forty-foot boat, for example, you will need someone who can work the winches and jibsheets, someone who can steer, and (even with an electric windlass) someone with enough strength to deal with anchoring. If the wind comes up suddenly, you can't steer and shorten sail alone.

If your entire crew is composed of experienced sailors—enough of them to handle the boat—your only considerations are where and when you want to go and how much it will cost. You are ready for any type of charter: bareboat, crewed, or flotilla. The options are somewhat more limited for a less experienced crew.

Bareboating, the ultimate in sailing freedom, is for the experienced crew. The boat is yours for the period of the charter and you go where and when you want. Psychologically, it provides the greatest feeling of accomplishment: you (collectively, that is) have done it on your own. An alternative, even for an experienced crew, is a flotilla charter. In most cases you will have enough free-sailing days (you can check this out when you first contact the charter operator) to allow you the feeling of independence, but you also get the camaraderie of other cruising crews. And if you or your crew are inexperienced or nervous about cruising, the flotilla concept may be the perfect solution. A crewed bareboat may be the right choice if you want to totally relax while cruising the area you selected, or if the folks in your group are inexperienced and need the help of a professional crew. The easy life on a crewed bareboat is not hard to take. It's just hard to give up at the end of the trip.

You also need to consider the accommodations you will want. The crew and their ages and relationships will be a major deciding factor. Think in terms of sleeping arrangements, number of heads, and so forth to keep everybody happy. An all-female or all-male crew may require somewhat different arrangements than a mixed crew. You don't have to worry about accommodations appropriate to the area and climate, because the charterer will have taken care of that for you.

Finally, let's get down to the charterer. Chances are there will be more than one charter operator in the area you select. There are several questions to answer in making your selection. Does the charter operation encompass the area you are interested in sailing? How long has the company been around? While longevity does not necessarily mean one operator will be better than another, it is always good to look at the track record. Can the company provide any references? The size and type of boats available is an important consideration. All things being equal, the larger the boat you can swing—either in terms of cost or crew—the more you will probably enjoy the cruise. The larger boat provides more privacy, more space to store your belongings, and less feeling of being on top of one another, whether in the cabin or up on deck.

The contracts issued by charter operators are usually very straightforward and generally very similar, although some are more detailed than others. Some operators also provide a booklet or pamphlet that explains the contract provisions in detail.

The contract will normally include the following: specific identification of the boat model and size; the time period for which it is chartered; cost, including insurance deposit; the charterer's limits of insurance liability; when the deposit will be returned; equipment on board and food provisioning; the promise by the operator to provide a boat in good working order with fuel and water; details of the operator's responsibility, should there be a delay in providing the boat at the time contracted for; geographic and time-of-day sailing restrictions, if any; the charterer's cancellation privilege and penalty for exceeding the time provision; the charterer's right to either withdraw the charter or include a paid skipper, should sailing competency of the charterer prove to be inadequate; the charter operator's disclaimer of responsibility for any swimming or diving injuries; who pays for port, customs, or dockage fees, if any; the charterer's responsibility to return the boat at a specific time and place with the boat in good condition and clean; any customs papers (if required) in good order.

Nothing complicated and nothing you would not expect. In fact, it tends to be less complicated than many auto rental contracts. Be sure you understand all terms before signing.

Cost may be another variable when selecting a charter. If one charter operator is considerably cheaper than another for a comparable boat, it is a good idea to delve deeper to find out why. Generally, similar boats at the same time of year in the same area will be pretty close in price. Look into exactly what is included in the total cost and what extras the charterer may offer, such as cheaper airfares, side trips or tours, and land accommodations. The charterer will usually spell out in the literature sent to you what is "special" about their operation.

Organizations such as BOAT/U.S. (880 South Pickett Street, Alexandria, VA 22304–4606) or magazines such as Cruising World or Sail also offer crewed or flotilla charters. These generally vary in time and location from year to year. One feature frequently available on these charters is the celebrity participants who either sail along or are met along the way. Celebrities may include famous sailors whose books and magazine articles you may have read. They may be specialists in the area you're sailing or well-known circumnavigators, racers, sail makers, or gear experts. Their presence adds another dimension to the cruise.

If you have special requirements (such as a wheelchair, unusual travel arrangements, or specific dietary needs), contact your charterer early. Remember, they're in the service business, and, with few exceptions, they will go out of their way to provide what you want and need. On your part, keep your requests within reason. While charter operators attempt to accommodate your requests, they cannot customize everything for everybody or there wouldn't be enough time for their normal activities. But you can usually count on them to cooperate whenever possible and to do whatever they can to make your charter a success. It only makes good business sense, because they want you to spread the word among your sailing friends about what a good time you had and they want you to come back.

Planning Your Charter

There are a number of details you have to take care of before you leave on your charter, especially if you are traveling to a foreign country. This is also the time to do all the planning that will add enjoyment to the cruise both before and during the trip.

Legal and Health Requirements

For travel to a foreign country, be sure that you and your crew have up-to-date passports. Depending upon where you live, this can require some time to obtain, so don't wait until the last minute. The charter operator will usually tell you if visas are needed. If the operator doesn't specifically tell you they are not required, check and make sure, since they can take a while to procure.

In a foreign country (particularly if you are bareboating), you will usually be required to present a crew list (name, age, address, and passport number of each person aboard) several times during the cruise. In some ports only the skipper will be allowed to get off the boat until all is cleared. It's much easier, less time consuming, and less expensive to make photocopies before you leave and carry enough for when they are needed. Even after you check into a country, some ports will ask you to present a crew list in addition to your crew's passports.

A call to the health department or your personal doctor will let you know which, if any, inoculations are mandatory in the area you are visiting and which are advisable. These standards may change from time to time, so don't assume because you've been to an area before that the same health requirements stand. Check this out early because you may have to start taking pills well in advance of the trip (for example, pills to prevent malaria). Don't

think "It can't happen to me." It makes sense to use a little pre-
vention rather than to ruin a trip or to find when you return that
you brought back an illness or disease. The charterer will inform
you of local no-no's, such as impure drinking water or any foods
to stay away from.

Transportation

In some cases the charter operator will make flight arrangements
for you or help you to make them. If not, this is a detail that
should be atteneded to as far in advance as possible. You may well
be flying during a peak traffic period in which many people have
made reservations. Don't wait until the last minute only to find
out that you can't get a flight at the time you want or that you and
your shipmates can't travel together on the same flight. There are
enough unexpected problems that come up, so take care of the
things you know about in advance.

Speaking of unexpected problems, if you plan to cruise
among the Windward Islands of the Caribbean, a word of caution
is in order. You will probably arrive at your original destination by
LIAT, which is the small, government-controlled airline. LIAT

The *Coral Trekker*, a 75-foot Norwegian-built square rigger, plies the
waters of the Whitsunday Islands and Great Barrier Reef (*Ashley Kerr,
Coral Trekker Sailing Safaris*)

stands for Leeward Island Air Transport, but frequent travelers to these islands swear it stands for Luggage In Another Terminal. LIAT's planes are small, none seating more than twelve to fourteen passengers, yet the airline has a propensity for misplacing your luggage. You will undoubtedly receive it the next day, but be forewarned: Carry hand luggage with essentials such as toiletries and a change of underwear. We had one comical night with nothing except what we were wearing.

Ground transportation at your charter destination will nearly always be arranged by the charter operator. If the operator doesn't mention it, be sure to inquire. Getting to and from your home airport is your responsibility. And just a bit of advice that may sound unnecessary: don't forget to arrange when and where to meet your shipmates. It's surprising how many trips start out with people racing around airports trying to find their travelling companions because they didn't work out this detail ahead of time.

Trip Insurance

When you schedule a charter, the last thing you think of is the possible need to cancel it. Still, things can happen—illness, accident, business emergency. Many charter operators, as well as your own insurance agent or American Express, offer trip insurance. Trip insurance is usually composed of three elements, and you can choose any or all: trip cancellation, medical and accident insurance, and lost baggage. These are not standardized policies, so it is necessary to look into the specific coverage offered.

The trip cancellation or interruption aspect insures you if you must cancel or interrupt your trip. However, it must be for specific reasons covered by the insurance, such as illness or injury to one of the people covered, a major disaster at home, or an airline strike. Some will also insure you if your charter operator can't deliver the boat for some reasons. It is up to you to read the fine print to determine what is covered and what is not, and whether it then makes sense for you.

Baggage insurance covers lost, stolen, or damaged luggage and personal effects. This may well be covered by your airline or even your homeowners insurance, so check this out before opting for the coverage. Medical and accident insurance provides coverage for treatment of illness or injury, usually including a "hot line" for medical availability in foreign areas. This may also include emergency transportation back home. Again, read the policy carefully to see what is and is not included. Only you can determine whether trip insurance is worthwhile for you. Insurance for a two-week trip will probably cost somewhere in the neighborhood of $160 to $200 per person.

Planning the Cruise

One of the most enjoyable parts of a cruising adventure can be all the dreaming and the planning you do, while still at home, about the places you will visit and what you will do there. The charter operator will usually send advance charts of the area. These are not the detailed charts needed for navigating and piloting, which the charterer always provides with the boat, but charts adequate for trip planning. Sometimes the charterer will also provide a sailing guide. Chances are that a cruising guide has been written for the area. Most large marine stores and some large bookstores carry cruising guides, and your local library is likely to have information on the area you intend to cruise.

Before leaving you will want to plan an itinerary. You may well change the itinerary after being briefed by your charter operator, or you may decide to revise it during the cruise itself. Nevertheless, planning your trip is not only enjoyable, but it helps to assure that you will hit the high spots of the area, as far as you and your crew are concerned, rather than learning about them at the end of the cruise.

Cruising guides go into a fair amount of detail on the sailing area, ports, anchorages, and sights to see. They provide information on the size of towns, their facilities (restaurants, banks, hot showers, etc.), and the availability of food, water, fuel, and marine supplies. They also tell you about the local currency. Importantly, the guides also describe the anchorage itself—whether you can anchor out or tie to a quay, whether this is usually stern-to or bows-to, whether it's a good all-weather anchorage or if winds from a certain direction make it uncomfortable (or even dangerous) as an overnight stop. Some places will be described as great for dropping the hook and having lunch or swimming or snorkeling, but lacking in sufficiently good holding ground to consider as an overnight stop. Headings, ranges, and landmarks will often be described to guide you into a harbor and into the best position for anchoring.

One important caution in reading guides to anchorages: Read these directions but check them with your charter operator to make sure conditions have not changed. Even with that done, keep alert when going into a strange harbor or bay. Navigational aids are sometimes missing, and shoreside features can change. If possible, have one of your more knowledgeable crew members in the bow, ready with prearranged hand signals for port, starboard, reverse, and stop.

As mentioned, navigational aids are not always where they are supposed to be. Neither are rocks or coral. So pay careful attention when entering a strange anchorage. If coral or rock abound, come in with the sun behind you so that you can "read" the color of the water where danger lurks, allowing you to navigate safely. Polarized sunglasses help immensely. Keep an eye on your chart, compass, and depth finder, and come in slowly. In wide open areas or ones that I am familiar with, I'd just as soon sail in rather than motor (I like to sail). In an area unknown to you, however, the ability to control speed and direction under power is a tremendous safety factor.

Keep in mind that you are on a cruising boat, not a racer, and plan your cruise itinerary accordingly. Measure your distances not only along the shoreline and between islands, but also into and out of harbors. In some areas the wind is quite predictable both in speed and direction, while in other areas you have no way of knowing. Also, tides and currents and their effect on the boat vary greatly from one place to another. If you are going to make an error in time estimates, you're better off allowing a little more time than not enough. Remember that, except in rare cases, you won't be sailing when it's dark. As a rule of thumb, use three knots as your average boat speed. Consider your shipmates when planning the length of a day's sail. A seven- or eight-hour sail might be acceptable to them once during the cruise. Would they be happy if this occurred several times during the trip? Maybe so, but maybe not. As skipper it's your responsibility to see that you have a happy crew.

Taking the helm *(Whitsunday Rent A Yacht)*

Also as part of planning the cruise, consider what you think you will want to do at each destination. If it's a restaurant or some nightlife you're looking for, you can afford to arrive a little later in the day. If you plan to anchor and then take the dinghy over to an area for snorkeling, you will either want to stay overnight and snorkel the next day or arrive with enough daylight left to allow you to snorkel that day. Consider, too, whether you will be able to anchor overnight near the snorkeling area or will need to move to a more secure anchorage *during daylight*. The charter operator or local residents will be able to let you know about dances, shows, ceremonies, or other events you might be interested in attending.

The cruising guides will give you a pretty comprehensive view of an area and allow you to schedule places and events. In all probability you will make yourself a fairly tight schedule. That's fine as a preliminary plan, but don't be rigid. You may fall in love with a place and decide that you want to spend more time there, or learn of a side trip that will make you want to lay over an extra day. You're on vacation, not on a tight business schedule, so relax. Wind and weather can also be a great changer of plans. A long slog on a beat due to a wind shift may make an alternative port much more appealing. If an intended anchorage is getting hit by wind, you might consider some other destination. And it can be a lot more fun exploring a town or the nooks and crannies of a particular taverna than sailing in an all-day rain. It's simply amazing how a taverna becomes increasingly cozy as the weather deteriorates.

In summary, pre-planning your cruise accomplishes a number of things: It helps to assure that you will see and visit the areas and sights that are of most interest to you rather than miss attractions of special interest; it helps to organize your time; it helps to assure that all of your crew's interests will be taken into consideration; and it provides an enjoyable activity before leaving.

Crew Assignments

If you are going with an experienced crew, allotting assignments is probably not necessary (except perhaps for the matter of who will cook). An experienced crew usually alternates at different jobs such as raising or reefing sails, handling the tiller or wheel, tending jibsheets, anchoring, and securing the dinghy. Still, it can be helpful to assign some responsibilities ahead of time so that certain primary functions will be accomplished with the least amount of scrambling around. These jobs might include checking the bilge, daily pumping, oiling the diesel gland, turning the propane tank on and off, making daily radio checks, and juicing up the batteries. These are daily required jobs that can be accomplished with greatest efficiency—without any one person being overburdened—by giving each person specific ones to perform.

With an inexperienced crew it is particularly helpful to discuss assignments in advance. It allows a novice sailor or first-time cruiser to know what will be expected of him or her. It also gives individuals the feeling that they are participating in a meaningful way. Be sure to let them know that any chores they are not familiar with will be carefully explained by you. If you can practice some of these things on your own boat prior to the charter, so much the better.

Keep in mind the physical requirements when you assign a specific job. Handling the anchor, tailing the jibsheets, and hauling the halyards require some physical strength, while checking the radio or turning on the fuel tanks for the stove do not. Most raw crew members are anxious to learn something about sailing, so you may want to plan some time during the cruise when you can show them various aspects of boat handling and seamanship. This makes the cruise more interesting for the crew and provides you with more hands when a job needs to be done. Rotating the same job among crew members gives each individual a broader base of knowledge and experience.

Crew assignments help assure that when something needs to be done, it will be accomplished in the smoothest way possible without any disputes as to who does what.

What to Take with You

Packing for a cruise involves two types of decisions: what to bring, and what *not* to bring. Nearly all of us, for example, end up taking way too much clothing. Sensible planning of the clothing, toiletries, and other personal gear we take along can make for a more carefree cruise.

Let's get one subject out of the way immediately. *Under no circumstances take any firearms or illegal drugs.* This has nothing to do with morality. It would be bad enough if customs authorities caught you trying to bring drugs or weapons into a country. They could, at the very least, make things extremely unpleasant. But if you were able to smuggle the contraband into the country and were then caught with it aboard the boat, they could confiscate the entire boat. (This is the case in the United States as well.) It isn't worth even considering. Don't do it!

Now down to the things you *do* want to take, beginning with personal items. You will want toothpaste, toothbrush, floss, electric razor with an international recharger (or a blade razor with shaving cream), deodorant, comb, soap, and shampoo, plus other personal toiletries you would take on any extended trip. It makes sense to bring sunscreen; the sun can be surprisingly potent, and the reflection off the water adds to the potential for sunburn. Bring some form of analgesic (such as aspirin), medication for stomach upset, and insect repellent.

Bring some facial tissues and toilet paper (many places have toilet tissue that could be substituted for sandpaper). You might want to bring an oral antihistamine, which can reduce swelling from insect bites in addition to its standard function as a decongestant. Remember any specialized items you need, such as wrist or ankle supports. Bring any prescription drugs you need; it might be advisable to also bring a prescription from your doctor. A few small adhesive bandages, a pair of tweezers, a small pair of scis-

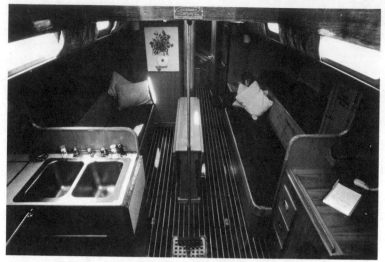

Main cabin of the *Ecstasy*, a 42-foot Hinckley *(Proper Yachts)*

sors, and antiseptic should round out your medical needs (the charter operator should also provide a complete first-aid kit with the boat). It makes sense to check with your shipmates on some of these items, since you don't each need to carry, for example, medication for upset stomach—but you do want to be sure that one of you has taken it along in case it's needed. You can't take for granted that you will be able to buy these items where you are going, especially if you prefer specific brands. Even if they're available, they can be costly.

If you wear prescription glasses, it is good insurance to bring along an extra pair plus a copy of your prescription. Sunglasses are essential, and if they are polarized they can help cut the glare off the water when you're trying to "read" it for rocks and coral. It pays to wear some kind of retaining strap to keep glasses from falling off. Nothing can foul up a trip faster for someone who wears prescription lenses than to have the last pair fall overboard. Straps or devices are available that will keep the glasses afloat should they fall overboard.

Deciding what clothing to bring is probably the toughest part of packing. Many people take clothes and changes for just about any contingency—then end up not wearing a large proportion of it. We lug a heavy load to and from the trip, sometimes sacrificing space that could have been used for stuff we really needed or for items we pick up during the cruise. Some boaters carry less and less each cruise, but still carry more than they need.

Except on rare occasions, we don't need dress clothes on a cruise. In locales where we want to adhere to the local dress code, we might not wear shorts or bathing suits ashore; a simple dress or a pair of slacks (even jeans) will generally suffice. The more you take, the heavier the load you have to carry, the more you have to unpack and store aboard, and the less room you have for souvenirs or gifts to bring back with you. The more you carry, the more you can count on the fact that whatever you want to find is going to be on the bottom of the bag.

Even if you don't normally wear a hat, bring one along. You will probably be exposed to the sun for extended periods, and often to a sun far more intense than you are used to. A hat with a brim will help avoid a burn and can also help prevent headaches caused by sun exposure. You won't have laundry facilities much of the time, so bring enough underwear and socks to carry you through a good part of the trip. Socks can help you avoid having your insteps burned by the sun. Include an old T-shirt to wear to avoid sunburn when you snorkel or swim for extended periods. Bring two pairs of jeans, a pair of shorts, and a bathing suit. You will undoubtedly spend a good deal of your time wearing the shorts or bathing suit. Bring along a sweater, light jacket, or sweatshirt for the cool evenings. A foul-weather jacket can be helpful not only aboard ship but as a raincoat ashore.

Bring a good pair of boat shoes for traction on deck. Another pair of shoes, suitable for walking, is helpful for going ashore. This allows you to keep your boat shoes on the boat, away from shoreside sand and grit that might later be ground into the deck of the boat. An old pair of sneakers is useful to protect your feet when you swim or snorkel around coral, sharp rocks, or sea urchins. Sea boots (high rubber boots with soles that provide traction) are bulky and take up a fair amount of room in the duffel bag, but they can come in handy during heavy rain or if the deck is awash in rough seas. There hasn't been a trip when I haven't used them.

A sharp sheath or folding knife always comes in handy aboard ship. Towels are not usually provided, so bring some with you.

And what are you going to carry the clothing and personal items in when you leave on the cruise? A hard-sided suitcase has no business on a small sailboat; there's just no place to store it. Ideal is a duffel bag which can be rolled up and stuck in a small space after you have unpacked. The soft sides also allow you to squeeze in some of the "extras" we all remember at the last moment or seem to pick up on a trip. If possible get a bag that is waterproof, or at least water repellent, so your clothing won't get wet if it's raining, or if the bag is set down in a puddle or sprayed while being transported in the dinghy. You wouldn't want to start out a trip with wet clothing, particularly if it's salt water (chances are it won't dry out during your entire trip).

Years ago I invested one dollar in a denim bag with a shoulder strap. Today it would undoubtedly cost a great deal more (even though it doesn't bear a "designer" name). This turned out to be a wise investment. The bag has gone along on every cruise. When you go ashore there is always a certain amount of paraphernalia you want to bring along. Rather than filling your pockets or carrying around an armful, take a small backpack or some sort of bag that can close and that has a shoulder strap to leave your hands free.

You also need some way to carry your cash, traveler's checks, and passport with you when you go ashore. Most money belts are very limited in how much they can carry. Wallet-size holders are available, however, that are large enough to contain cash, traveler's checks, and passport. They have a loop so that you can put a belt through it, and wear the "wallet" inconspicuously inside your shorts or jeans. In most places that you anchor or tie up, you probably don't have to worry about theft aboard. But a wallet of this type helps to prevent problems and worry on shore.

A few other items can help make your trip safe and more enjoyable. Bring along a small high-powered flashlight that fits in your pocket. You will be surprised how many times you go ashore thinking that you will return in daylight, only to end up returning in the dark. It also comes in handy aboard ship. Even if you are not a photography buff, bring a camera. You're sure to see sights you will want to view again and be able to recall long after the cruise is over. Sending photos back to people you meet on the trip can help you maintain contact long after the cruise. Bring film, since you will generally find it less expensive than buying overseas. Charter boats usually come with a pair of binoculars aboard, but they often are pretty banged up. If you already own a pair, bring them along. Don't forget a couple of inexpensive pens and the addresses of the people you want to send postcards to.

To further enhance the cruise and help recall it afterward, bring along a small notebook and keep a daily log—not the nautical kind, but a record of what you do each day, including anything of particular interest or any incident that amused you. Record the names of places you've seen and of people you've met. When you return from your trip, you can type up the log and send copies to all your shipmates. They will appreciate it, and when you read it yourself in later years, the whole trip will come back to you.

Add your passport and your flight tickets, and you're packed!

Part Two:
Where to Charter a Sailboat

Chartering around the Globe

One of the tremendous advantages of chartering is the opportunity it gives a sailor to skip all over the world without taking the time or trouble to sail from one area to another. Not that cruising from one area to another isn't fun, but if you don't have a lot of time, yet you want to cruise in the eastern Mediterranean and then sail the Florida Keys, you can do it the easy way: you fly from one area to the other. You don't have to transport a boat to a new area in order to enjoy a cruise there.

There are so many places to go and so many places to see, and chartering offers a way to go and see them. This chapter briefly describes some of the world's major chartering areas. We'll start with the United States and then shift to major cruising areas in other parts of the world. Later in this book, we'll go into more detail on most of these areas—and we'll introduce some fascinating cruise locales that may come as a surprise to you.

United States East Coast

I'm not sure that anyone really knows the number of islands along the coast of Maine. The area has more than its share of fog, but the delightful scenery, the ability to gunkhole (that is, to pull into areas just to look around) in numerous harbors and coves, and the quaint downeast villages make it an extremely popular sailing area. (Incidentally, it's called downeast because prevailing winds set you sailing downwind when going east.) You can sail the Maine Island Trail, a 300-mile-long waterway for small boats, running from Casco Bay in the west to Englishman Bay in the east. Or you can cruise Penobscot Bay and spend weeks exploring picturesque islands, taking short or long sails as the whim hits you.

Heading south on the eastern seaboard, you come to another prime cruising ground, Chesapeake Bay. More than 200 miles long, Chesapeake Bay provides top-notch sailing and fishing plus an array of historic towns, modern seaports, lazy waterfront villages, and maritime museums. Farther south is North Carolina with Pamlico and Albermarle sounds and the Outer Banks. The area abounds with history, from Blackbeard to the Civil War. The sounds tend to be shallow and the rivers deep, inviting some exciting exploration. The town of Oriental alone boasts more than a thousand resident boats. The area offers a large number of secluded anchorages along with southern charm.

Proceeding farther south into subtropical weather, you reach the Florida Keys, a narrow chain of islands ranging 125 miles southwest from Miami to Key West. The area provides some of the best fishing, snorkeling, and diving in the world. Unlike some of the more northerly areas, the Keys have a climate suitable for sailing any time of the year.

United States West Coast

Off the coast of the state of Washington lie the San Juan Islands, ending just short of the mainland Canadian border. The San Juans are the tops of a prehistoric mountain range. The scenery spans a wide range from evergreens to cactus, with prolific wildlife. Many of the islands offer excellent hiking trails. Some of the islands have docks, and some provide free mooring buoys on a first-come, first-served basis. Numerous unpopulated islands with quiet unspoiled coves enhance the popularity of this area for cruising. Crossing over into Canadian waters is simple, with fast and courteous customs clearance.

Dropping down the west coast, you can charter out of either Los Angeles or San Diego. From L.A. it is a pleasant sail over to Catalina Island. Sailing into Avalon Harbor, you can pick up one of the moorings, but you have to get there fairly early in the day— it's a popular area. The cobblestone streets of Avalon have a flavor of Mediterranean villages. Going up the northern coast of the 21-mile-long island, you can anchor at Isthmus Cove, where launch service is offered. About one-third of the way down the southern coast is Catalina Harbor. Wild buffalo still roam the island.

From San Diego you can head out to Mexico's Coronado Islands or take a short trip south to Ensenada, Mexico, where you

The *Ecstasy* under sail off St. John, U.S. Virgin Islands *(Proper Yachts)*

can either anchor or grab a mooring buoy and then take a water taxi. Sailing around San Diego itself is interesting, tooling around San Diego Bay, Harbor and Shelter islands, and around Point Loma up to Mission Bay. The weather permits sailing all year, but chartering is most popular from April through October. In late fall and through the winter, the area can be hit with powerful Santa Ana winds.

The Caribbean

Just 170 miles from Florida—stretching to the southeast in a string of more than 700 islands and 2,400 cays—are the Bahamas. At the closest point is a wonderful thousand-square-mile bay bounded by Great Abaco and Little Abaco islands to the west and more than 100 sandy cays to the east. These natural barriers keep out the heavy ocean chop, while allowing very dependable trade winds to blow through. The crystal-clear water allows you to sail for weeks without losing sight of the bottom of the bay. Farther south in the Bahamas, you can charter out of Eleuthera Island and head down to the Exumas. Magnificent snorkeling and excellent fishing, as well as dozens of snug anchorages, are available within the 22 miles of the Bahamas National Trust Exuma Land Sea Park.

The British and U.S. Virgin Islands lie east of Puerto Rico. The British Virgins—far less commercialized and with fewer large cruise ships—tend to be favored by sailboat cruisers. The area offers sheltered sailing with short hops from island to island or from one harbor to another. The Virgin Islands offer some of the best snorkeling and prettiest beaches in the world.

The Windward Islands, one of the best sailing areas in the world, lie farther south down the Caribbean chain of islands. From Martinique and St. Lucia in the north to Grenada in the south, just above Trinidad and the tip of South America, is this string of islands offering gorgeous scenery, lovely beaches, wonderful snorkeling, and dependable east-northeast winds of fifteen to eighteen knots day after day. The Tobago Cays offer what some say is the best snorkeling in the world. Grenada is one of the lushest islands you can imagine, with a picture-perfect port at St. George's Harbor.

The Mediterranean

Prime cruising grounds in the Mediterranean include Turkey, Greece, the French island of Corsica, and the Italian island of Sardinia. (The former Yugoslavia was also becoming one of the more popular cruising areas in the Mediterranean, but current hostilities have made chartering in this region unavailable and unadvisable. We will reserve coverage of the area for future editions of this guide.) Each of these areas offers tremendous variation. The Lycian coast on the southwest side of Turkey offers a rugged shoreline with the remains of ancient cultures everywhere—Greek, Roman, and Lycian. You can easily see where one culture added alongside or on top of the other cultures in various ruins that remain in remarkably good shape. Ports vary from swinging towns with bars and restaurants and excellent shopping to uninhabited islands where wild donkeys live. You can take side trips to see Lycian rock tombs, to visit other ancient sites, or to soak yourself in odoriferous but soothing sulphur baths.

Across the Aegean Sea lies Greece, where the Sporades Islands present a variety of contrasts from picturesque towns to unspoiled wilderness. Many of the villages seem to be from the last century, with donkeys carrying their loads through cobblestone streets. Nearly every island has tavernas where you can stop

Ionian sunrise

for a cool drink or have dinner, often with a wonderful view of the harbor. In Greece's Saronic Islands, you have easier and shorter sails. Swinging around Greece to the west, you go from the Aegean Sea to the Ionian Sea, where the islands seem to be vertical, with the village usually perched on top. Some of the islands have caves at water level, some big enough to hold a small yacht.

The islands of Corsica and Sardinia are geographically close but culturally far apart. Corsica is very French and never lets you forget that a guy named Napoleon was born there. The food and restaurants are excellent, but quite a bit more expensive than in Turkey or Greece. Sailing to the southeast of Corsica, you reach two lovely uninhabited islands, the Lavezzi Isles, with beautiful anchorages and crystal-clear waters. Just a little farther southeast you arrive in Sardinian waters and the La Maddalena Islands. From there you head south to Palau and fabulous Costa Smeralda and Porto Cervo. While Corsica is very French, Sardinia is very Italian.

This chapter has introduced some of the world's major cruising areas. But there are hundreds more, some of which will be described in subsequent chapters. After your first cruise, the problem becomes how to get to as many of these wonderful places as possible. It's a great problem, and well worth trying to solve!

Four of the Most Popular Chartering Areas

Now that we've taken a brief look at major chartering areas around the world, let's get down to more detail. This chapter will be devoted to four of the most popular chartering areas, with specifics about each. These are not necessarily the easiest areas to sail (those will be covered in a subsequent chapter), but they are extremely popular and offer a variety of sailing conditions.

The Bahamas

The beautiful Bahamas offer pink-white beaches, wonderful sun, and excellent sailing, snorkeling, and fishing. This archipelago of more than 700 islands and 2,400 cays southeast of Florida is easy to reach from the U.S. east coast. The name Bahamas comes from the Spanish *baja mar,* which means "shallow waters." The water tends to be deeper at the northern end of the Bahamas and shallower as you head south. Because it is so shallow, you get spectacular sea colors of blue and green, with truly breathtaking hues as you head into shallower water. The tradewinds blow reliably all year. There is little variation in daytime temperature, which averages eighty degrees from spring through fall and somewhat cooler in the winter (average of seventy). A light sweater in the evenings makes it very comfortable. The capital of the Bahamas is Nassau, on New Providence Island. Nassau is a major resort area and one of the key offshore banking areas in the world. The area has a colorful history extending from the landing of Columbus on San Salvador Island, through the days of piracy, prohibition, and gun runners, to the more recent drug trade. The numerous isolated islands and cays make for some easy-to-hide spots.

At the northern end of the chain are the Abacos. The Sea of Abaco consists of about a thousand square miles of sheltered

Cruising Bahamian waters *(Easy Sailing Yacht Charters)*

waters, with Great Abaco and Little Abaco to the west and more than one hundred sandy cays sheltering the east. The Abacos (also known as the Family Islands) offer more than seventy harbors, crystal-clear waters, delightful villages, and exciting reefs for snorkeling. Bakers Bay on Great Abaco has wonderful snorkeling. Farther around Great Abaco, on the eastern side, is an anchorage hard to surpass in beauty, Little Harbour. Marsh Harbour on Great Abaco Island is the third largest town in the Bahamas.

From Marsh Harbour you can head northeast to Man of War Cay and North Harbour, where you can visit Edwin Albury's boatyard, which still builds beautiful wooden Bahamian boats. North Harbour also affords good shopping for supplies, heavy canvas hats, jackets and bags from Albury's Sail Loft, a good bakery, and a restaurant featuring local foods (you can eat conch prepared any number of different ways). Just a little south of here is South Harbour, a lovely, tranquil spot to anchor. The land around South Harbour is privately owned, so don't go ashore, just enjoy the lovely setting.

From South Harbour, head up to Scotland Cay and then to Great Guana Cay, where you will find mile after mile of gorgeous sand beaches—and an excellent restaurant. Still farther north is Green Turtle Cay (aren't the names great?), with a very good harbor at New Plymouth. In New Plymouth, you can shop for souvenirs and provisions and try any of several restaurants, including the New Plymouth Inn, built around 1860 and specializing in local dishes. For an evening out, sail to Treasure Cay, which has one of the leading resort hotels and an excellent restaurant. For a quiet anchorage, go to Fowl Cay and stay over for the spectacular snorkeling.

Approximately 30 miles northeast of Nassau lie Eleuthera Island and its surrounding cays. Eleuthera is about 90 miles long and features steep cliffs, caves, and pretty beaches. If you sail southwest from Hatchet Bay on Eleuthera's southeast arm, you can go through Current Cut between the southwest end of Eleuthera and Current Island and on to Royal Island. As you near the cut, take a look at Eleuthera and you should see a rock formation called the Glass Window, two cliffs that drop into the sea and are joined by a natural bridge. At Royal Island you will find a secluded, well-protected anchorage.

The next day, you can sail east to the island of Spanish Wells. Most people living here are descendants of Eleutherans and British Loyalists who arrived during the American Revolution. The island's name stems from its discovery by the Spanish in the seventeenth century and the further discovery that the island provided excellent well water. The pretty village of Spanish Wells, with colorful houses and gardens, has a number of stores. If you decide to go to Harbour Island to the southeast, hire a local boat pilot for the day (about $25 to $30 U.S.); this reef-strewn area is known as the Devil's Backbone, and it's not advisable to sail here by yourself. Harbour Island is one of the leading resort areas in the Bahamas, but it remains pretty much unspoiled. Dunmore Town on Harbour Island is one of the oldest settlements in the Bahamas.

Heading south in the Bahamas, you reach the Exumas, a chain of about 365 islands (sail to a different one each day of the year). The area contains lovely beaches and very colorful waters, and consists of mostly uninhabited islands. You have to be somewhat more careful sailing the Exumas than the Abacos since the waters are shallower. If you like to fish, you can obtain a fishing license when you first clear customs for a fee of $10. The major town on Great Exuma Island is George Town.

West of Great Exuma is the Great Bahama Bank, a stretch of shallow water; to the east is Exuma Sound. Heading northwest you will pass Lee Stocking Island and Big Farmer's Cay before reaching Staniel Cay (also known as Staniard Cay). The quaint village there (the stereotype of the slow-moving native village) does have some shops. Across from Staniel you can see three islets. One of them contains Thunderball Cave, which provided the exciting underwater scenes in the James Bond thriller *Thunderball.* You can take your dinghy over and swim into the cave—it's truly magnificent—but, sorry, you'll have to supply your own gorgeous companion.

Farther up the island chain is Warderick Wells, one of the prettiest of the Bahamian islands. It offers a good anchorage and is headquarters of the Exuma Land and Sea Park, which lies between Wax Cay and Little Bell Island. Fishing is prohibited in the park. As a result, when you snorkel you will find some very friendly, colorful, and large fish, such as grouper, which are totally unafraid of you. There are also some pleasant nature trails to explore on Warderick Wells.

On Norman Cay, farther northwest, one of the more interesting events in recent history is documented by the remains in the bay of a large twin-engine plane, a former drug runner. On shore you can look at the remains of an old Medellin Cartel smuggling headquarters. There is also an excellent reef for snorkeling, patrolled by barracuda that seem to ignore you. Continuing up the archipelago you reach Allan's Cay and its pretty beach. The bay and the reefs off the island have good snorkeling with a wide variety of friendly and colorful tropical fish. The fishing is also said to be quite good. On the island you'll periodically hear hisses; iguanas, protected by law, are all over Allan's Cay.

Visitors to the Bahamas can take advantage of the People-to-People Programme offered by the Bahamas Ministry of Tourism. It permits you to get together informally with local residents for such activities as picnics, teas, exploring the island, learning about local cooking, or dining at a resident's home. You explain your interests and the program makes the arrangements. For information contact the Bahamas Tourist Office or the Manager, People-to-People Programme, P.O. Box N-3701, Nassau, Bahamas; (809) 326–5371.

The best period for sailing the Bahamas is from December through June (the hurricane season runs from July to November). There are daily flights from Florida to Nassau, Freeport, and George Town, as well as frequent interisland flights.

Greece

For a totally different type of venue, try Greece. Wherever you go you will find the people extremely friendly, especially on some of the smaller islands that can be reached only by small boats and have not been inundated with tourists. As a result the people really are glad to see you. You will find English spoken by many, and with just a few Greek words you can get along fine. In addition to excellent sailing, lovely scenery, and friendly people, chartering in Greece gives you the opportunity to see evidence of antiquity just about every place you turn. Daytime temperatures are in the mid-sixties in April, the mid-seventies in May and October, and range (on average) from the mid- to high eighties from June through September.

Ionian Sea

We'll start in Homer's "wine-dark" sea, the Ionian. Up north is the island of Paxos, known for its olive oil. Olive trees grow wherever you look—along the road, between houses, you name it. Paxos is a quiet, hilly island (nearly all of the Ionian islands seem to go up and down as much as horizontally). In the small village of Gaios is a square bounded by a church and several tavernas; in the middle of the plaza are tables and chairs for outdoor dining. Tavernas, which offer drinks and food, are a fixture of Greek towns. About a block away is the hardware store, where you can also change money since it doubles as the bank. Along the shore is a small post office. You can do your provisioning at the village's surprisingly well-stocked little grocery store with the help of very friendly storekeepers who either forgive your mangled Greek or speak to you in English.

If you motor out of the north pass from Gaios and then come onto a 140-degree heading, you're aimed for Mongonissi, a picturesque island with fantastic limestone formations that look like a regiment of frozen soldiers. You can sail nearly all the way into the bay, drop a kedge (an auxiliary or second anchor) from the stern, and put a bow line on shore. Then hop over the side for a swim and dry off at the taverna right on the beach as you sip whatever you feel like sipping. If you walk to the end of the islands, you can see beautiful natural limestone "steps" on the opposite shore and get a nice view of the next island, Anti-Paxos, with limestone, olive trees, and an occasional cactus surrounding you.

Sailing east to the Greek mainland, you will reach Parga. You approach the well-sheltered Parga Voltos Bay between a church and an old Venetian castle high on the headlands and tie up to the quay. You can get to town two ways: by water taxi (for about 40 drachmas, or approximately 60 cents) or by walking (a nice half-hour hike around the bay, along the beach periodically adorned with topless bathers, across a couple of small creeks, and up the mountainside on a rock and dirt path). Before going to town, visit the old castle, quite interesting and with a fabulous view: a small island with an old white church and a graveyard that takes your breath away as you look at it from your high vantage point.

You reach Parga by walking down a long and wide winding stairway, perhaps the picture you had in mind when you first thought of Greece. Parga includes lots of restaurants and tavernas, stores for souvenirs, and a wonderful bakery. The kebob, mokos (small fish), and baklava in Parga are great. It is not unusual for a restaurant owner to entertain you by playing the mandolin or leading some dancing (they really do dance in the aisles). If you intend to walk back to the boat, take a flashlight since you will probably stay longer than you intended and the walk back over the mountain and small streams can be quite an adventure in the dark.

As you sail south toward the island of Levkas, there is no way you would know by just looking that a canal lies ahead. It looks as if you're heading for shore, but a sudden dogleg to starboard, with an old citadel off to port, and you're in the canal. You have to motor here—the canal is only about fifty yards wide with extremely shallow water on either side. The canal was dredged to a depth of seventeen feet in 1946. You can see the potential for problems by viewing the beached rusting freighter below an old fort to port, but the canal is well marked with stakes. At the end of the canal you're in among the Ionian Islands. About halfway down the island of Levkas is the good-size town of Nidri. You can drop anchor right in front of the town, where there are numerous tavernas, stores to buy provisions, hotels, a couple of excellent bakeries, and places to buy gifts.

From Nidri you can sail past Moodra, around Sparti, and then south past Aeropidi and Skorpio, all owned by the late Aristotle Onassis. Take a look at the beautiful beach cabanas on these islands. Continue south to the island of Meganisi. At the northern end is the picturesque waterside village of Port Vathi, where the homemade natural yogurt with cucumber at the Rose Garden is fantastic. Hike up a steep switchback to the definitely non-tourist village of Katomeri. The baker's wife came from Houston, Texas. As you walk around, you feel as if you have gone back in time.

Farther down the coast is the nicely sheltered harbor at Port Spiglia. The village of Spartahori is perched high on the hill. As you walk up to Spartahori and other villages, the vista surrounding you is magnificent. You will notice, as you go up the switchbacks, little shrines, often made of ouzo bottles filled with burning oil; these are frequently shrines to people who drove off the cliff in that area, and the contents of the ouzo bottle are often the cause of the accident. When you reach Spartahori with its narrow, winding, inclined streets, you would again swear you had gone back 150 years in time. Billy the Chicken is a favorite taverna, which sports photos signed by visitors including John F. Kennedy. The food is excellent, the atmosphere great, and Billy and some of his older patrons will usually demonstrate Greek dancing for you.

Spartahori, Greece

The "phone company" is housed in a small old house with wooden pillars: one phone on a table, with loads of exposed wires, and you dial direct—no waiting!

Two bays east of Port Spiglia is Abelike Bay, with an excellent beach for swimming. Heading southwest you pass Arkudi and then reach the island of Ithaca, the home of Odysseus. Halfway down the island is the Gulf of Molo, with two small ports, Kioni and Frikes, at its head. From Frikes you can visit the reputed hometown of Odysseus, Stavros, the ancient capital of Ithaca. Sailing farther south in the gulf, you head west into about a three-mile-long bay at Port Vathy with deep water up close to shore. From here you can sail around the northern tip of Ithaca and west to Fiscardo on the island of Kefalinia and tie up at the quay; the tavernas are right there.

Next sail north to Vasiliki Bay on the southern tip of Levkas. You can't really see the harbor until you get nearly all the way in. You'll find a lovely little village. You will be surprised at all the ancient "rubble" you find in the grass here and on many of these islands, crumbling walls and sculpture you would give your eye-teeth for that are just lying around, slowly giving way to the elements. But don't touch them; it's illegal. From Vasiliki you can take a bus, for about 15 drachmas, to the village of San Petros—basically one long steep street that has not yet been touched by the tourist trade. (The police chief's brother lives in Detroit, and he himself speaks perfect English.)

From Vasiliki you can sail over to the southern tip of Meganisi and explore the water-level caves. There is a story that during World War II, a German sub used one of these caves as a base. You can dinghy into some of these caves with thirty-foot-high entrances that are sixty to seventy feet wide. The caves increase in size as you go farther in, showing stalagmites, rock "windows" and "doorways," and tiny beaches. Head up the western side of Meganisi and into Levkas Town, a good-size town at the northern end of Levkas Island.

Much of the sailing in the Ionian Sea is in fairly sheltered waters with land (islands or mainland) surrounding you, forming a large baylike area. The sailing is easy and the sights rewarding, two of the reasons it is among the most popular chartering areas.

Saronic Islands

Still in Greece but farther east toward the Aegean Sea and southwest of Athens are the Saronic Gulf and the Gulf of Argolis. Here are the Saronic Islands and the Peloponnesian peninsula. With somewhat more wind than you will find in the Ionian Sea, the area is still pretty well sheltered and offers easy sailing. You can start from the tiny village of Korfos and sail south to Epidavros, which lies at the foot of the Peloponnesian Mountains. During the summer you can take a taxi to the historic theater of Epidavros, where Greek actors still perform ancient dramas. From here it is an easy sail to Angistri Island, where you can drop the hook and go for a swim while you wait for the afternoon breeze to pick up. From Angistri it is a short sail to Poros, a bustling little island that is quite cosmopolitan. The town of Poros, perched on a volcanic outcrop, is a busy tourist town with an active nightlife. You'll be in for a pretty sight if you walk to the top of town in late afternoon or early evening, to the small chapel next to an old windmill, and watch the sun set over mountains and bay.

To the south, you'll come to Hydra Town, on the island of Hydra, with houses climbing step-like up a steep hill, and narrow cobbled lanes and steps everywhere. Hydra is a swinging town with a disco as well as the usual tavernas and quayside cafes. You can swim off the rocks in front of the harbor wall. You'll enjoy the sight of donkeys carrying their loads of straw. Northwest of Hydra is Ermioni, a small fishing village with huge groves of olive and lemon trees. All through Greece you will see olive, eucalyptus, cypress, lemon, and pine trees, looking great and giving off wonderful fragrances. You can walk to the other side of the village to a bay where snorkeling is quite good. For a change of pace and a little solitude, sail across to Dhokos Island, which is uninhabited or has only a couple of families (it depends on when you get there). Several quiet coves offer good swimming and overnight stops. Heading west you reach the last of the Saronic Islands, Spetsai. The village is fun to walk around in. They still build fishing caiques here, and other than moped or bicycle, horse-drawn gharries are used for transportation. Along the northern shore you come to a large bay with little white churches at each end; this bay has particularly clear water and offers good snorkeling.

Across from Spetsai on the mainland is a large village, Port Heli, with an almost landlocked bay, one of the best natural harbors in all of Greece. Farther up the western mainland coast is Khaidhari, a deep, quiet inlet good for overnighting. There are a couple of small tavernas ashore. Continuing west you will reach Tolon, which is now a tourist area because of its nice beaches and proximity to ancient archaeological sites. The harbor is quite small. Just north of Tolon is Navplion, which once was the capital of Greece. Here you'll find a large harbor. You can climb up the one thousand steps (count them) to the thirteenth-century Venetian citadel.

Still farther south is Plaka, with a small harbor and three tavernas ashore, a long white pebble beach and very clear water, and a dramatic backdrop of mountains. Three miles inland, which you can reach by taxi, is Leonidhion with its narrow winding streets. A twenty-minute taxi ride takes you up a steep road to a Byzantine monastery, now a convent, built into the cliffs; it's half cave and half building. The nuns there will gladly show you around, and the overall view is awe-inspiring. Down the eastern shore of the Peloponnesian coastline is Kyparissi, where you will find a large bay, surrounded by mountains, with a sleepy little village at its head. About 11 miles south is Yerakas. Watch for the entrance by looking for a light on the headland, then enter a narrow passageway between sheer cliffs into a perfectly sheltered harbor. The village is quiet and unspoiled.

Nine nautical miles south of Yerakas, you reach Monemvasia. You can tie up at the quay north of the causeway, which connects old and new Monemvasia. A ten-minute walk from the quay brings you to the portal entrance of the town. Known as the Gibraltar of Greece because of a similarity in topography, the town dates back to Minoan times when the original fortifications were built. The present town was built during the Byzantine period and was a major commercial port. Much of the lower town has been rebuilt in the original style, with narrow winding streets. You can hike up the steep steps to the citadel in the upper town. Across the causeway on the mainland is the modern town of Monemvasia, with many stores and tavernas.

Sporades Islands

Farther north in the Aegean Sea lie the Sporades. Less sheltered than the Ionian or Saronic islands, the area features more wind and even better sailing in more open water conditions. If you intend to bareboat in the Sporades, you should have some experience. Starting from Orei on the island of Evvia, a small fishing village with a beach off the quay, you can head up the Oreos Channel and, at Cape Stavros, swing west to Pegadi Village and a taverna for dinner that evening. An ancient watch tower overlooks the harbor entrance. From here head east in the Trikeri Channel, with steep blue cliffs off to port and a fertile plain off to starboard. Stay near the northern shore until you pass Platania Bay and then aim for Koukounaries on Skiathos Island, where you can drop the hook for a nice swim. Then head south around the coast to Skiathos Town and tie up to the quay or anchor in the bay, a large sheltered harbor. A little islet joined by a causeway has good rock swimming. Skiathos Town offers a number of tavernas and shops, and is a quaint place to walk around.

It's an easy sail from Skiathos to Skopelos Island. Head southeast between the island of Arkakion and Tzoungria and then east to Panormos Bay, a good overnight anchorage. Then continue southward around Cape Miti and on to Velona Point. Stop at Staphilos Bay (on Skopelos Island) for a swim before proceeding to Skopelos Town. A very colorful town, Skopelos has tavernas and stores ranged along its narrow streets and alleys, and is well-known for olives, plums, and almonds. You can walk to the monasteries perched on the hills above town. Legend has it that some of the gold decorating these monasteries was a gift from the notorious pirate Barbarosa.

Alonisos Island is just east, with Patitiri slightly above the southeast tip. Anchor in the harbor since the quay is very small and usually occupied; just be sure you're not in the way of the daily island ferry. If you feel like a nice hike, take about an hour and a half to walk to the old fortified village high on the hill and walk around the old streets. Don't miss the view overlooking the sea. Just north of Patitiri is Stenivala, which will be your last chance for provisions before exploring some uninhabited areas.

Gunkhole in the coves along the east coast of Alonisos and

then cross over to Pelagos Island. In the south are several bays nice for swimming—especially St. Petros, which has crystal-clear water. You're on your own now—no tavernas or people. You'll find a twelfth-century monastery if you anchor at Monastery Bay. East of Pelagos is a small islet called Sphika, where you can snorkel and swim through arches of underwater stone. Then go northeast to Iura Island, inhabited only by goats and by the goatherd and his family; they'll show the way to Cyclops Cave, a huge cavern with stalactites. Iura is not good for an overnight stop, so head back to the northern end of Pelagos and the excellent anchorage at Planitis Bay.

From here head back down the east coast of Alonisos and drop south to the island of Skyros. The island is really in two parts—the north, with fertile valleys and many types of trees, and the south, pretty much uninhabited, with tall craggy peaks. The western coast has various bays, including one at the southern end that Saracen pirates used as a base back in A.D. 900: Tre Boukes, with its guardian islets of Platia and Sarakino. Halfway down the western coast is the main port of Linaria. Skyros Town, a fortified village perched on the side of a hill, with colorful houses, is worth a visit.

Turkey

A favorite, and very different, cruising and chartering area lies on the eastern side of the Aegean Sea. This is Turkey, which offers good winds, fabulous archaeological sights, fascinating scenery, and very friendly people. Daytime temperatures run from the high sixties in April to the seventies in May and October. It's warmer from June through September, ranging from eighty-four to ninety-one.

We'll start at the southwest tip of Turkey, in the western corner of the Gulf of Gokova at Bodrum, a large town with many shops and restaurants. In fact, it's known as the St. Tropez of Turkey. The castle of St. Peter, built in the fifteenth century by the Knights of St. John, has a museum of underwater archaeology displaying items found on area shipwrecks. Bodrum offers considerable nightlife and, like many Turkish towns, excellent buys in rugs and in leather goods from handbags to coats and jackets.

From Bodrum sail east to the small village of Cokertme. Many of the local people speak at least some English, and if not, a friendly "Merhaba" (hello) will be enough to break the ice. Several times we were surprised and amused to see crowds sitting around open-fronted tavernas watching "Dallas," dubbed in Turkish, on local TV. All along the eastern coast of the Gulf of Gokova are bays and harbors suitable for gunkholing and overnight stays. Gokova, in the westernmost corner of the gulf, is a good place to provision. Sail over to Castle Island and take a look at Cleopatra's Beach. The story is that Cleopatra had the sand imported from Egypt so that she and Anthony could romp on it (geologists have actually determined that the sand *did* come from Egypt).

Heading southwest down the main coast, you come to Yedi Adalari (*adalari* is the Turkish word for "island"), where you're sure to find a quiet and probably private anchorage. At the tip of the peninsula (Cape Krio) is Knidos, and you can head from there into the Dorian Gulf (also known as the Gulf of Symi), which is right where the Aegean and Mediterranean seas meet. Knidos, a relatively small village, had 70,000 residents in the fourth century B.C. Farther east is the small farming community of Palamut, with a couple of tavernas, followed by Datca, a lively little town where you can buy provisions, fill up with fresh water, and tie up for the night.

From Datca you can go east to Port Losta, drop a kedge off the stern, and tie up to the quay. Go up the stairs to the restaurant for dinner, and sit on the second-floor terrace for a lovely view of the harbor. In the morning walk around to the school, where you will see the children dressed in their black and white uniforms; in the 1920s Turkey adopted the French educational system, including its mode of dress, and hasn't changed it since. Next day head northwest to circumnavigate a fascinating fortress-like rock called Kopintha, and then head northeast into Penzik Bay. Think twice about going for a swim: Penzik Bay is reputed to be a breeding ground for sharks. Continuing east along the coast, stop for lunch in pretty Pedalo Bay and then proceed to Kiervasili for its safe overnight anchorage.

Next morning, continue down the peninsula to Cape Apostei. About 4 miles offshore you can anchor on the edge of a reef which eventually rises to just six inches below sea level

Heading toward Port Losta, Turkey

(check your chart and watch for breaking waves). Swim over and have someone take a photo of you having a "religious experience" as you "walk" on the water. Heading farther south, your next overnight stop is Bozburnn, where you will find a deep and well-sheltered inlet, good restaurants, and some nightlife, and will have an opportunity to buy provisions. In Bozburnn and in other towns and villages, you will see guillots being built. Guillots are pretty, clipper-bowed boats with junk-type sterns and short masts (though I never saw any sails, only motors). Because few hardwoods remain, the guillots are built from pine and last only three to five years.

From Bozburnn go out past Vunos Island, then southwest to Cape Valpes, farther south to Cape Alupo, and then east to Port Aplotheka (a total of about 20 nautical miles). About ten years ago the wreck of a Byzantine galley was discovered in nearby Serce Harbor, its ancient cargo of glassware still aboard. As you sail into Aplotheka, you'll see the ruins of a Greek fortress from 400 B.C. on the hill. Aplotheka is a multifingered bay. Pick a spot to drop your anchor and take the dinghy ashore with a stern line. Then climb up to the fortress, Loryma, walk around the ruins and the wide fortress walls, and take in the impressive view.

Continue north-northeast into Marmaris Fjord, which provides more than twenty square miles of sheltered water (although it can be a wet sail if the wind is in your face). Kumlubuku Bay has the area's best snorkeling. This area is the setting for the scene in C.S. Forrester's *Hornblower and the Atropos* in which Captain Hornblower evades the Turkish blockade. You could spend days sailing the fjord and its bays. Head east around Passage Island and into Marmaris Harbor. Marmaris is a large town with many tourists, hotels, condos, and lots and lots of boats. It is loaded with stores (great buys on onyx, leather goods, and carpets), and has a really swinging nightlife. It's worth going to Marmaris just to get a steak dinner at the Zhudum Restaurant—unmistakable with its purple tablecloths. The total tab, including coffee, was $3.00 to $4.00 per person. For less than $2.00 you can get a haircut that includes a head and neck massage. There is also a Turkish bath and massage parlor in town. The old part of town centers around a castle built in 1522 by Sultan Suleiman I that served as the staging area for his successful attack on the Crusaders at Rhodes. It's worth spending a day or so exploring various bays in the fjord, many of which, such as Nimaro, offer quiet and well-protected anchorages.

From Marmaris continue east, watching out for Edmond's Rock, about three-quarters of a mile offshore and only about a foot and a half below the surface. As you sail toward Ekincik, there is a small bay for a lunch and swim stop. Head into Ekincik, drop the anchor off the bow, and take a stern line ashore (it's too shallow to go in bow first). Next day you can take an exciting side trip up the Dalyan River. You can arrange to be picked up right off your bow by a guillot, which will then proceed to the shallow mouth of the river. (The skipper will probably have the fifty or so passengers aboard the guillot shift over to port or starboard so he can bump over the very shallow sandbar at the mouth of the river. You have to return when the tide is right or you can get hung up on the bar.) You will travel aboard the guillot among a maze of reed islands, with reeds up to fifteen feet tall, and in a very few minutes you completely lose your sense of direction. The boat stops at the ruins of Caunus, which dates back to 44 B.C. and includes a large amphitheater you can clamber around in, Roman baths with the pipes still in working order, and an altar with a beautiful setting. The boat then takes you upriver to a domed natural sulphur spring that is very warm, very smelly—and extremely soothing to sit in. Then you hop in the freshwater river to get rid of the rotten egg smell. After lunch at the village of Dalyan, you return to the guillot, which retraces its voyage and deposits you back at your boat.

If you decide to head south from Ekincik for a sail, stay at least 3 miles away from the island of Rhodes. Rhodes is Greek, and because of the antagonism between Greece and Turkey, your boat will be impounded if you are flying a Turkish flag. For a really nice long sail, about 42 miles, head south, then east and up Fethiye Bay to the head of the bay to Gocek, a small town with a few tavernas. We were once lucky enough to have dinner at one of the tavernas when the father of the bride (or groom; we never did get that straight) was giving a prenuptial dinner for his friends. The dancing, drums, and bouzoukis all going at once made it a very memorable and festive occasion.

Fethiye Bay is extremely interesting to sail around and gunkhole. There are a large number of inlets, some suitable for snorkeling. Some of the more interesting are Valley Bay, Boynuz Buku, Kapi Creek, Four Fathom Bay (with the ruins of a deserted village ashore), Wall Bay, Cold Water Bay, and Tomb Bay (where you will find more Greek ruins). Be sure to visit Cleopatra's Bay and explore the remains of what are purported to be Cleopatra's baths. A couple of miles inland you'll find the remains of a small Roman town. At Olu Deniz you'll see a lovely two-mile long crescent-shaped beach with a resort on the shore. You can circle Karaca Oren Adalari with its rugged rocks and intriguing ruins (with its deep water and lack of inlets, I never found a place to anchor or tie up so we could go ashore).

For a real treat, anchor off Gemile Adalari, which is farther east along the coast. Go for a swim off the boat or off the rocks ashore, then explore the island and its fascinating ruins—Greek (you can still see part of a mosaic floor), Roman, and Byzantine. You'll see the ruins of tunnels and buildings and on one arched wall the remains of a fresco of an angel, which the Byzantines tried to obliterate because they considered representations of the human body to be sacrilegious. If you see a donkey wandering around, pet her around the ears and pluck a few eucalyptus leaves for her to eat, and she'll follow you all through the ruins and around the island. She may also come down to the edge of the water at four in the morning and bray her affection for you (she promised to write, but you know these donkeys). Gemile Adalari

View from the ruins of Loryma, Turkey

is a nice overnight anchorage. One of the taverna owners will come over by boat and invite you to his restaurant for dinner. If you accept, he will pick you up in his boat at whatever time you wish and bring you back at the end of the meal. Then head back north and pull into Fethiye, a large town with many shops (you could buy a pair of designer sweats for $8.00) and many, many restaurants and tavernas, as well as a busy nightlife.

Dropping all the way south and then heading east along the coast you can pull into the deep bay at Kalkan, with many restaurants and tavernas along the shore and up the steps behind the village. From here you can also arrange to visit the ancient sites of Palara and Xanthos. Going still farther east you come to Kas, a small, pretty town with facilities for eating and provisioning. Finally you reach Kekova, where you'll find the remains of an ancient Lycian town, most of which sank beneath the sea during an earthquake. You can still see steps leading underwater to buildings below and, just above sea level, several stone sarcophagi. Good winds and open, deep water make for excellent sailing in this area. The entire area from Bodrum to Kekova is far more than you can explore in only two weeks. It might be better in three two-week segments, but whichever part you cruise, you'll never forget it.

San Juan Islands

For another popular chartering and cruising area, we go halfway round the world to the northwest coast of the United States and the San Juan Islands. This group of 172 pine-covered islands is bordered on the south by the Strait of Juan de Fuca and on the north by the Strait of Georgia. To the east is the state of Washington and the majestic Cascade Mountains and the southern border of Canada, and to the west is Canada's huge Vancouver Island. The area is quite sheltered, with best winds during the summer months. The San Juans offer excellent sailing along with scenery and wildlife that are hard to beat. Summer temperatures can range from as high as the eighties during the day to the fifties during the evening. The winds tend to be more reliable and a bit stronger in June and September, compared with July and August.

Washington state maintains seventeen marine parks throughout the islands, some of which have lovely hiking trails. There also are two national historic sites and eighty-four wildlife refuges. You may see seals, dolphins, a wide variety of birds including great blue herons and bald eagles, and if you're lucky, whales. While most of the islands are covered with evergreens, on Lopez Island in the southeast you'll see cactus.

Bellingham, Washington, is a good jumping-off point to explore the archipelago. Head southwest to Lummi Island, where you can either sail north through Hale Passage or around the southern coast of the island. Stretching northwest of Lummi are the islands of Matia, Sucia, and Patos. Be careful of the rocks and reefs around Sucia. Matia is not suitable for overnighting but is good for gunkholing. Sucia, on the other hand, has three good harbors for overnight stays: Echo Bay, Snoring Bay, and Fossil Bay. From here it is an easy sail south to Orcas Island, which contains some spectacular fjords, then south to Shaw Island and the seclusion of Parks Bay. Nearby Lopez Island has some good overnight stops. Next, take the short northwest trip to San Juan Island's Roche Harbor, where you can reprovision and find a restaurant in the bustling resort area. If you prefer more seclusion, head for Garrison Bay. From there sail to Stuart Island and deep, well-protected Reid Harbor. If you get there early enough, you can grab one of the public moorings maintained by the state. The price is right—they're free. In crossing over Spieden Channel to Stuart, be sure to check the tide. You may have to motor since the current going with the tide can reach four to five knots. There is a very nice beach at Reid Harbor, although the water is quite cool for swimming, and on shore are some pleasant trails. You can walk across the island to Prevost Bay. Stuart Island houses Turn Point Lighthouse, the northwesternmost lighthouse in the country. As part of your San Juan cruising, also try to head down to the Canadian city of Victoria on Vancouver Island. Clearing customs is painless and can even be done by phone at the customs dock. Victoria is a fascinating city with friendly people.

Seven Exotic Areas
You Can Charter

The world is full of exotic locales, and many of them make for fascinating cruises. We'll take a look in this chapter at a sampler of cruising areas that through rare beauty or striking features are truly exotic.

Thailand

Thailand is known as The Land of Smiles. This is not puffery or exaggeration. If you meet or see someone in Thailand and he or she doesn't smile at you, you find yourself wondering what's wrong. The Thai are the friendliest people I have met anywhere. This is also a wonderfully exciting place to cruise. Charters are quite new in Thailand, but the operators, to date, have been set up by experienced chartering organizations, which have ironed out glitches very quickly.

Chances are you will fly to Bangkok, a busy, sprawling city of over five million people. If possible allow a few days to see the sights. The Royal Palace—actually acres of palaces, temples, buildings, and sculptures—is one of the most fantastic sights you will ever see. You can take boat rides up the Chao Phrayo River and the klongs (canals) around the city to see private residences, the Museum of Royal Barges, and the Temple of Dawn. The river is filled with vessels, including "longtailed" boats that are 20 to 35 feet long and very narrow, with automobile motors fitted to a long shaft that extends about seven feet inside the stern and twelve feet astern at a very shallow angle. These boats really fly! They're used as freight carriers, fishing boats, taxis, and school buses.

See a Thai kick-boxing match one evening, and you'll get as much of a charge out of the crowd as the fight itself as the people chant in rhythm with the kicking. Shopping is good, the food the best I've had anywhere, and the city fun to be in with its prolific

Thai fishing boat

traffic. Taking a ride in a tuk-tuk, a sort of motorized rickshaw, is much more exciting than a roller coaster as all the mopeds, motorcycles, tuk-tuks, taxis, buses, and cars cut in front of one another; it's enough to make New York cab drivers feel they lead a quiet life. You can also take an overnight trip upriver on converted rice barges—beautiful teak craft converted for passengers, with lovely teak staterooms and candlelight dinner on deck (this ain't roughing it)—to see the Bang Pa-In Summer Palace, the famous Reclining Buddha, and (via bus) the haunting ruins of Ayutha, which was the Siamese capital from 1350 to 1767.

From Bangkok you can fly to Phuket and the sleepy little community at Leam Maphrao. You can sail north or south from here to equally enjoyable but very different areas. North are spectacular uninhabited islets and rocks, excellent holding ground, and muddy bottoms. South are sand and coral and clear water with some inhabited islands, including resort areas. One caution: There is a lack of large-scale charts for the area, and there are shallows and rocks as low as six-tenths of a meter (about two feet), so pay close attention to your depth finder. None of the islands have docks or quays. The monsoons in the area end in late October. Sailing is best from November through March. The temperature ranges almost year-round from the low nineties during the day to the mid-seventies in the evening. When it goes into the nineties it can get quite muggy ashore.

While you are at Leam Maphrao, take a 1-kilometer walk to Mai Khoa Thalong, a small, definitely nontourist village with rubber tree plantations, papaya trees, and coconut palms all over. Everyone smiles and waves to you, and the children throw shy smiles over their shoulders as they giggle. As an example of the hospitality of the people, we stopped to admire a parrot outside one of the houses. Ali, the homeowner, invited us to come closer and told us about the various birds there, then ran up a coconut tree and brought down two coconuts and lopped off the tops with a machete so that we could drink the milk, and then cut out the coconut meat for us to eat. Meanwhile, we were surrounded by about a dozen grinning and laughing children. Ali then introduced us to his wife, infant daughter, and brother. It was a warm and spontaneous reception, typical of the Thai people.

You need to provision because most of the islands in the area are uninhabited. Be sure to buy loads of fruit; the pineapple, papaya, mango, grapefruit, oranges, and bananas are the sweetest I've ever tasted. Leaving Leam Maphrao you can dip down around the headland and sail north into Phangnga Bay and some spectacular scenery, a cross between a lunar landscape and Monument Valley with water. There are islands, islets, and just plain rocks of grotesque shape rising out of the water, some as high as one thousand feet or more and most with sheer cliff walls complete with stalactites. As you leave Leam Maphrao, the water is very shallow in places and requires careful piloting and close attention to the depth finder. As you get farther north the water becomes deeper—twenty-three to thirty-seven meters, right up to the walls of these islands—but you still have to watch out for shallows. Anchor off of Ko Phunak (*ko* is the Thai word for "island") for the night. Chances are you will be the only boat around except for local fishing boats whose loom of lights you will see as it gets dark. Many of these boats have banks of powerful lights to attract fish, and even when you can't see the boats directly, their lights float over the islands. Bring insect repellent for the no-see-ums with voracious appetites.

Next day sail close to Ko Phing Kan. The James Bond film *The Man with the Golden Gun* was filmed here (remember the plane flying among those fantastic rocks?) and, in fact, the island is now also known as James Bond Island. It's too shallow to sail near the shore, but you can anchor and take the dinghy over and walk up the steps to the cave that Mr. Bond traversed. From here sail south among the maze of islets and head for the west side of Ko Hung to a small bay. Be sure to check for rocks not just around your anchor but in a full circle around the boat. The holding is excellent, but you can't see the mud bottom without swimming around. Even with a bottom check, a wind shift caused us to start pounding on a rock in the wee hours of the morning and no amount of anchor-line maneuvering could stop it. We finally had to haul up the anchors and tack back and forth over a quarter-mile course that we knew was safe until it was light enough to see.

As you head south from here the bottom turns from mud to sand and the water becomes greener and clearer. Drop anchor at Ko Mai Phai, a breathtakingly beautiful island with a lovely beach. This is the best site in the area for snorkeling and is excellent for swimming. From here head over to Ko Phi Phi, said by some to be one of the three most beautiful islands in the world. (It's very pretty, but the description is somewhat overstated.) Anchor in the bay on the southwest coast. A small resort ashore offers lunch, dinner, and drinks, and a couple of small gift shops. If you walk the attractive sand beach in the evening, you'll send hundreds of sand crabs scurrying.

Approaching Ko Phunak

As you sail around you will see an amusing sight: cigar-shaped fish about eight to ten inches long that, when scared, take three slapping bounces on their side and then "run" vertically on their tails along the water for fifty to seventy feet, using their tail as a scull. I'm sure that if they were not invented by Kodak, they are at least on contract—but you'll need a fast hand and a long lens to capture them.

Swing down the coast of Ko Phi Phi and sail east to Ko Phraya Nak. Large caves on the island are filled with birds' nests, which the locals collect to make soup. Round the southern end of the island and sail up the west coast across the channel back to Ko Phi Phi, then head past your previous anchorage to a large bay on the southern coast. There are palm trees everywhere, and three-fourths of the bay is ringed with white sandy beach. You have quite a vista: steep mountains in the distance preceded by forest, then palm trees, the curving white beach, and clear, green water.

Ashore is a busy little village with hotels, cottages, restaurants, gift shops, and so forth, many of which look to have been hastily built. You'll encounter young backpackers from England, Sweden, France, and Germany. You'll see local fishermen caulking their longtail boats and kids scampering up trees to get coconuts.

On Ko Phi Phi and other inhabited islands, you'll see pet gibbons, which are the smallest of the apes and the most acrobatic. They're playful and love to grab your hat or eyeglasses. Most have to do some work for a living; they are taught to pick coconuts and bananas.

Now head northwest for the channel between Ko Yio Yai and Ko Yai Noi, keeping a close lookout for the (unmarked) deep-water channel between the islands, and anchor in the shelter between the two. From here it's about a seven-hour southwest sail to the bay at Ao Chalong. The bay looks like a wide-open anchorage going in, but there is an unmarked sandbank smack in the middle, so go in slowly. Use your depth meter since the sandbank shelves sharply, but if you're going slow you won't get hung up even if you hit it. Go in a little too fast and you will have to either rock the boat off or kedge it off. You have to anchor about one mile offshore in the long bay due to the shallows. Take the dinghy in and tie up to the long, rickety dock (watch the loose and missing boards as you walk, particularly in the dark), and then take the exciting taxi ride (half paved road, half holes and dirt) to the large resort town of Patong Bay.

This is a bustling town of large hotels, many shops, and restaurants. The food is great. Most of the restaurants have fresh or live fish in tanks outside, and you simply point out what you want for dinner.

Next day take one of the local buses into Phuket Town, a smaller version of Bangkok. In Phuket Town we found a restaurant for lunch with 144 items on the menu, good enough that we came back for dinner. It cost $2.00 for each of us, including beer and coffee or soda—and we had food left over.

Tahiti

When most of us get bitten by the sailing bug and start to dream of faraway places, probably the one cruising area we all think of is Tahiti. Gauguin's Tahiti is long gone. The people are much more sophisticated and the area more citified than when he went to paint there, but it's still a beautiful place and offers excellent sailing. Tahiti is the biggest island in the leeward section of the Society Islands. The largest town and also the capital of French Polynesia is Papeete. While Papeete has to some degree been westernized, once you get a few miles out of town you still see the legendary lush vegetation, mountains, rustic villages, and waterfalls.

The entire area provides the scenery most of us associate with the South Pacific—the jagged mountain peaks, calm lagoons protected by barrier reefs, gorgeous sunsets. From Papeete you can sail west to the lagoon at Raiatea and then cross over to Tahaa. From here it is a short sail to fabled Moorea. If you head east you visit Huahine, which has some interesting archaeological sites. To the west lies Bora Bora. The hurricane season runs from November through April. The best time to cruise this area is May through October, when the winds are steadier and temperatures tend to be somewhat cooler.

Galapagos Islands

For the ultimate in exotic, try the Galapagos Islands. These islands are truly unique, containing animal and plant life found nowhere else on earth, leading Darwin, on his famous voyage in the *Beagle*, to establish his theory of evolution. The islands are owned by Ecuador, and cruising in the area is tightly controlled to assure maintenance of the unique flora and fauna. The entire Galapagos archipelago is a national park.

Only crewed bareboats and an occasional flotilla charter are available for the Galapagos. The islands, quite close to one another, give you the opportunity to see real live "dragons" and other animals totally unafraid of being approached. You really need a crewed charter to appreciate the area. The skipper will be not only an accomplished sailor but also a guide to the area and knowledgeable about the animals and plants. The best time of year to visit is December through May, since it cools off considerably during the remaining months due to the Humboldt current.

Venezuela

At the southernmost end of the Caribbean Sea is Venezuela and the area known as the Pearl Coast, or Costa Margarita. Pearl oysters were prolific here, and when the Spanish first arrived in the sixteenth century they took a fortune in pearls. The islands are quite close together and make for easy sailing. Puerto La Cruz is a busy tourist area with all the normal tourist attractions. Less than an hour's sail away are two pretty islands, Isla Monos and Isla Cachicamo. From here lie a profusion of islands within easy sailing distance of one another. Snorkeling is great among the coral, with a tremendous number of colorful tropical fish. The islands also contain parrots (so be careful what you say) and monkeys.

Much of the island area is a national park, which helps retain its natural state. Six-mile-long Mochima Bay displays fjord after fjord. You'll find a crescent-shaped beach perfect for swimming, sunbathing, or strolling on Isla Chimana Segunda, along with a nice cantina. Isla Borracha (which translates as Drunken Isle) has a very good harbor for overnighting. Farther north is another lovely island and major resort area, Isla Margarita. You could spend many weeks exploring the islands clustered between Isla Margarita and the mainland. December through April are the best times to cruise this area, with the least chance of rain. The daytime temperatures are fairly stable year-round, from the high seventies to around ninety.

Canary Islands

Off the Atlantic coast of Morocco lies another on our short list of exotic sailing areas, the Canary Islands (whose name derives from the word "canine," not from the canary bird). There are few navigational hazards because these islands belonging to Spain rise right up from the sea, but there can be very strong winds, particularly on the windward coasts exposed to the northwest trades. Winds and temperature remain pretty constant throughout the year. Day temperatures range from sixty-five degrees in the winter to eighty degrees in the middle of summer. It can get cool at night and when sailing between islands.

Unlike many of the areas described previously, the distance between islands often requires sailing overnight. Seven primary islands stretch from La Palma and El Hierro in the west to Lanzarote in the east. Due to the distances involved and the wind direction, which could entail some fairly intense beating into the wind, you probably can't cover all of the islands in just two weeks. In the past there were few harbors suitable for anchoring in the Canaries, but a number of harbors have been built in the last few years to accommodate cruising boats.

Tenerife, just west of the center of the chain and the largest island, is a major resort area with many stores, large hotels, and lots of nightlife. Tenerife has the highest mountain in the Canaries, 12,200-foot Pico de Teide. There is an excellent harbor at Puerto Colon. Heading around to the western coast, you can make a lunch stop at Los Gigantes but it's not suitable for an overnight stay. From here head northwest about 30 miles to La Palma, which is a very steep island, and its main harbor at Santa Cruz. A large fishing fleet is based here. Sail south to Puerto Tazacorte next day for lunch. Then head south to El Hierro, an overnight passage. There is a good harbor at La Restinga, where hills form a backdrop to the village. You'll delight in the graceful sheer and colors of the local fishing boats and the lovely Spanish influence in the architecture.

Now head northeast about 20 miles to La Gomera, where you will find three nice harbors: San Sebastion, where the ferry comes in; the fishing port of Playa de Santiago; and Valle Gran Rey, with sheer cliffs rising to terraced plateaus, one of the prettiest ports in the Canaries. For nice hiking and fabulous views, go up some of the cliffside roads on the island. To the east lie the islands of Gran Canaria (with a major port at Las Palmas), Fuerteventura, and Lanzarote (which convinces you of its volcanic heritage just by looking at it).

Finland

For another fascinating cruising area, charter in Finland, Land of the Midnight Sun. Off the southwestern tip lies an archipelago that is well charted and marked. You have your choice of short sails or longer cruises among the labyrinth of islands. Marinas and restaurants are sparse, so you'll do a fair amount of cooking aboard. This is more than compensated for by the magnificent scenery. Some strong winds blow between islands, so be alert when sailing between landmasses. The best temperatures and the most daylight for cruising are from June through mid-August. Temperatures run in the seventies during the day and are considerably cooler in the evening.

You will probably start from Turku, which is the business hub of this part of Finland and an international seaport. Just offshore is the tiny village of Nagu and its small marina. From here sail about 20 miles south to Berghamn. You'll sail among a maze of islands, with all channels well marked. The scenery is stark but appealing. Most of these islands are privately owned, but Finnish

Off Vuokra Veseto, Finland

custom allows their use as long as you don't abuse the privilege and if you leave them the way you found them. At Berghamn you can tie up to the dock and walk around the rustic village. Swimming is strictly optional. You're at sixty degrees north latitude, so the water is, at the least, brisk. From here you can head to Jurmo, a great sail, about 20 miles southwest. Jurmo stands guard over the southwest tip of Finland, defending it from the Baltic Sea. Head back toward the mainland and pull into the dock at Gullkrona, where you can buy freshly smoked fish. Sail next to Hango, a small sailing resort, and then to the coastal towns of Naantali and Tammisaari.

Seychelle Islands

For a truly different area to cruise in, try the Seychelles, a group of more than 100 islands in the Indian Ocean, east of Kenya and north of Madagascar. The Seychelles are home to giant land tortoises and other rare animals. In order to avoid damage to the environment, a number of the areas have been made national parks. The water is very clear, with excellent snorkeling among the coral reefs and heads. Most of the islands are uninhabited. At present, as in the Galapagos, only crewed bareboat charters are available. May through October is the best period for chartering. Temperatures don't vary much year-round, though the monsoon (rainy season) runs from November through April.

Three of the islands—Mahe (the main island), La Digue, and Praslin—have limited tourist accommodations. The capital, Victoria, is on Mahe. The harbor at La Digue is extremely pretty. On Praslin you will find something really striking: the 800-year-old palm trees (Coco de Mer Palms) at the Baie St. Anne. From Praslin you head to Bird, Fregate, and Denis islands. The beaches are spectacular. Even where there are tourist accommodations, the law prohibits a hotel being built higher than the palm trees, in order to help preserve the naturalness of the islands.

The Five Easiest
Areas to Charter

This chapter describes areas that are easy to charter in terms of navigation, piloting, and distances between ports. This should not discourage consideration by seasoned sailors: Easy does not mean undesirable. Every one of these areas can be enjoyed equally by veteran sailors and novices alike. For those who are considering their first charter, however, these areas present the easiest sailing and, therefore, are excellent choices.

Chesapeake Bay

Cutting deep into the heart of Maryland and extending down to Virginia is one of the finest cruising areas in the United States, Chesapeake Bay. More than 200 miles long, it offers fine sailing, top-grade fishing, and everything from major cities and towns to isolated anchorages in numerous coves, creeks, and rivers. The best time of year for cruising the area is late May through October.

Start at Kent Narrows, at the northeast end of the bay, north of Chester River. Here you'll find complete marina facilities, restaurants, and a dock bar. From here, head southwest around the point and then north until you reach the Chester River to starboard. Sail up to Chestertown, with its eighteenth-century aura, where they celebrate the "tea party" with a festival each May. Next head down the river and across Chesapeake Bay to Annapolis, the Maryland state capital, for a change of scenery. You can visit the Naval Academy and walk around the historic district. There are loads of shops and restaurants in Annapolis and a very active nightlife. Sail southeast and head over to St. Michaels, which is perhaps the most popular and best known anchorage on Chesapeake Bay. A visit to the Chesapeake Bay Maritime Museum is a must. The restaurants are good and, of course, feature fresh fish and shellfish from the area; try the crabcakes! Interesting stores cater to those in a shopping mood.

Swing farther south, still on the east side of the bay, and pull into Oxford. This former colonial seaport is a quaint town with eighteenth- and nineteenth-century homes and shady sidewalks. Very nice custom boats are still built here. Now head southwest over to Solomons, which has the Calvert Marine Museum, ship's stores, antique and crafts shops, and boutiques. Between Kent Narrows and Oxford are wonderful places to gunkhole and to spend a quiet day or night.

Well below Oxford, the bay widens out. You could stay on the west side of the bay and head up the Potomac River, eventually reaching Washington, D.C., where you could visit your tax dollars. Toward the east side of the bay are two islands, Smith and Tangier, where authentic Chesapeake Bay watermen still live. Down the coast are many deep coves, rivers, and creeks to pull into for either temporary or overnight stops, and small waterfront villages that seem to have stopped in a time warp. Mobjack Bay, toward the southwestern end of the bay, could easily take a week or more to explore.

Florida Keys

Off the southeast coast of Florida are the Florida Keys, a string of islands stretching for about 125 miles in a crescent-shaped curve to the southwest. With clear water and coral reefs, the keys are excellent for snorkeling and are one of the leading sportfishing areas in the world. The subtropical temperature (sometimes rising to tropical) makes it appealing year-round. The attractions of the keys (islands) range from mangrove jungles to bustling tourist areas.

Sailing is easier going from north to south due to the prevailing northeasterly winds. Except for watching out for coral (easy to do because of the exceptional water clarity), there is virtually no navigation involved at all in the keys. The distances you sail are strictly up to you, since you can find suitable anchorages at either close range or farther afield. The Florida Keys are an excellent choice if you are a little short on time and want to spend a week or less cruising, but still want to get that cruising feeling.

At anchor in the Florida Keys *(Caribbean Soul Charters)*

The northern keys tend to be good places for anchoring but not for going ashore. Bring insect repellent—the mosquitoes wear napkins. There really are three different cruising routes you can choose. On the eastern side of the keys is a string of reefs, now clearly marked but a graveyard for boats in the early days of sail. You can sail on the eastern side of the reefs in the Florida Straits; the fishing is great, but there tends to be a lot of traffic, commercial as well as recreational. Or you can sail down Hawk Channel, which lies between the reefs and the keys. The channel provides ample depth for sailing and is also well marked, and you benefit from the shelter of the reefs much as you would from an atoll. Or you can sail down the western side of the keys, but the water is quite shallow and sailing requires care; if your draft exceeds four and a half feet, this route is not advisable. Bridges along Route 1, which connects the keys to one another, open for boats and allow crossing over from the Gulf to the Atlantic at various spots, so you're not locked into one side or the other.

At Key Largo you must visit the John Pennykamp Coral Reef State Park, an underwater fairyland of fish and coral. The next key, a little farther south, is Islamorada, actually a string of five keys stretching for about sixteen miles, which boasts the only living coral reef in North America, a lovely beach, and a tropical hardwood forest (the Lignumvitae Key State Botanical Site). Islamorada offers free trolley service for getting around onshore. All through the keys you will find restaurants and stores. Farther south, about midway down the keys, is the major tourist and fishing area at Marathon, and at the western tip is Key West, which blends modern hotels with houses that look as if they were brought from New Orleans or New England. Several museums and historic house are open to the public.

British Virgin Islands

It's easy to list the virtues of the British Virgin Islands, in the Caribbean east of Puerto Rico: perfect weather, clear turquoise seas, tropical fish of every variety and color, steady easterly to northeasterly winds, and islands and harbors close enough to require only eyeball-piloting. Daytime temperatures range from the high seventies to about ninety degrees, making these islands desirable anytime of the year. You may need a light sweater in the evenings.

Tortola is a good starting point. Head over to Cane Garden Bay on the western coast of Tortola, one of the prettiest harbors you will see anywhere. Sail next to Sandy Cay, where you'll find great snorkeling and a lovely beach. From here it's a short sail to the small island of Jost Van Dyke for a first-rate lobster dinner. Green Cay, just to the east, is nice for a swim. Then head for Beef Island and an overnight stop at Trellis Bay. If you eat in the restaurant at Trellis Bay, you may discover a rather strange drinking

Total relaxation in the British Virgin Islands (*Proper Yachts*)

companion—a donkey named Chocolate who periodically sticks his head into the dining area and swills any beer you offer. (But don't let him kid you; he never buys a round.)

For the next leg of your cruise, head east past West Dog and the unfortunately named Cockroach Island and drop the hook at George Dog Island for a swim followed by a leisurely lunch on board. From here, sail past Seal Dog and head for Drake's Anchorage on Mosquito Island, one of the prettiest in the British Virgins. Long Beach on Mosquito Island has extremely clear water and coral gardens surrounded by a reef. The snorkeling is spectacular, with an enormous variety of tropical fish and coral.

From Mosquito Island, swing southeast to Virgin Gorda, where you can explore the caves, swim in underground pools, and soak in the famous baths, natural pools heated to bathtub-like temperatures. Your next stop is downwind, to Manchioneel Bay on Cooper's Island, where you can anchor near the beach and then dinghy over to Diamond Rock for some more terrific snorkeling. Sail east from here to Salt Island and swim over the remains of the *Rhone,* wrecked here over 150 years ago and now home to many tropical fish. From Salt Island it's a short southwest hop to Peter Island and the lovely anchorage of Deadman's Bay, where you should anchor in the northeastern corner, which is sheltered by a coral reef; again, crystal-clear water and excellent snorkeling. Go ashore for dinner at the resort area, where cruisers are allowed to use the beach chairs gratis.

On the following day, it's time to head downwind for another excellent harbor, The Bight, on Norman Island. Buried treasure from a Spanish galleon, the *Nuestra Señora,* was discovered here in 1750. Norman Island is said to have been the model for Robert Louis Stevenson's *Treasure Island.* From Norman it's a beam reach back to your starting point at Tortola.

Windward Islands of the Caribbean

In the southern Caribbean is one of the best sailing areas in the world, the Windward Islands. With the exception of Barbados, there's nothing between the Windward Islands and Africa except the Atlantic Ocean. The Windwards run from Martinique down to Grenada, almost off the tip of South America. The eastern (windward) side of the islands can have some pretty rough sailing, so most cruising is done on the Caribbean (leeward) side. Even on a two-week cruise you could not do the entire chain of islands with enough time to enjoy them. You might think in terms of two segments: Martinique to Bequia (a segment that includes St. Lucia and St. Vincent), and St. Vincent to Grenada. The Windwards should provide one of the best sailing vacations you'll ever have. The daytime temperatures year-round are about eighty to ninety degrees, with evenings dropping into the seventies. The best time for cruising is from December through May to avoid the rainy season.

Navigation is straightforward line-of-sight, with the next island always visible. However, you do need piloting skills to find some of the harbors. Care has to be taken going into many of the harbors due to coral heads and reefs, but the water is clear and easy to "read" by looking at the change of color. There are very few navigational hazards, and these are well delineated. There is one exception: the Tobago Cays require extra-careful piloting. But even with this cautionary note, the Tobago Cays are not to be missed. It's a place you'll never forget. Prevailing winds in the Windward Islands are northeast to east and run about fifteen to eighteen knots pretty consistently from fall through spring and about twelve to fifteen knots in the summer. The winds are almost continual, so even on a hot day it feels pleasant.

Martinique

Though you may start your charter from one of the islands farther south, we'll discuss the islands traveling from north to south. First, Martinique, which is more French than France. Over many years the English and French fought for possession of these islands. Martinique is part of France and the people don't want you to forget it. It helps if you know at least a few words in French. If you attempt to communicate in French, your reception will be much warmer.

Martinique is the largest of the Windward Islands. About one-third of the island's population lives in the cosmopolitan town of Fort-de-France, on the southwest corner of the island. It has an easy harbor to go into, but it does have a fair amount of traffic. Anchor southwest of the ferry dock, making sure you leave room for the passage of other boats. When you dinghy over, tie up at the largest of the ferry docks at Anchorage des Flamands, where you will be out of the way. This is a swinging town with good entertainment at night and wonderful restaurants. There are excellent shops in Fort-de-France (it's a free port), and it is easy to provision here. Shopping in the covered markets can be fun. It's a pretty town with pretty people. (Napoleon's Josephine came from Martinique.)

Martinique and many of the other islands are lush, with beautiful, sweet-smelling foliage and flowers. One caution, however: Martinique and some of the other islands have manchineel trees bearing what appear to be small green apples. Don't eat them or even touch them. They are poisonous, and even if you merely stand under the tree and sap drips on you, you'll blister. The trees are not a major hazard as long as you are aware of them.

Unlike most of the Windward Islands, there are no really good anchorages on the western coast of Martinique, which is dominated in the north by 4,800-foot Mount Pelée. Heading south there is an anchorage with a pretty beach at Grand Anse d' Arlet. From here head south and then east, staying north of Diamond Rock, where the British once managed to get cannons and troops up to the top to blast away at French shipping. The English commissioned the rock as if it were a ship of the line. Sail over to St. Anne, which provides good overnight anchoring and a beautiful beach. Experienced sailors can continue around the southern tip of Martinique and up the eastern shore to various anchorages, but it can get rough, plus the shoreline is full of rocks and becomes a lee shore (you get blown toward it).

St. Lucia

Just south of Martinique is the island nation of St. Lucia. If you're heading down from Martinique, you must clear customs at Castries on St. Lucia. (If you are heading north from St. Vincent, you clear at Vieux-Fort on St. Lucia.) It is essential that you clear in and out of each independent island or group of islands before going ashore. The harbor at Castries is excellent. It is a large town with fine restaurants and good shopping. Head north from Castries to Reduit, with its lovely mile-long beach, and anchor

Marigot Bay, St. Lucia (*courtesy of The Moorings*)

overnight. From there it's a short sail to Pigeon Island, which is joined to the mainland by a causeway. Anchor just offshore of the mainland. On Pigeon Island you can climb up to the ruins of Fort Rodney, from which the British devastated the French fleet. Head back south past Castries and gunkhole into Grand Cul-de-Sac Bay. There's a pretty beach, but the anchorage is too rolly for overnighting. Just a short distance south is Marigot Bay, ringed by steep hills, palm trees, and mangroves. This is a good place to stay overnight and also to go snorkeling.

Your next stop on St. Lucia is Soufriere, where you will either need to use bow and stern anchors or to drop the kedge astern and put a bow line ashore due to wind and current. You can take a cab to the sulphur springs and the Diamond Mineral Baths for an indoor or outdoor bath. There's also a pretty waterfall there. Now, just a short sail south, comes one of the most dramatic anchorages you'll ever see, the Pitons at Anse Des Pitons. The Pitons are two mountain peaks, Petit Piton to the north and Gros Piton to the south. The water is very deep right up to shore, so sail almost to shore, drop a stern anchor, and tie a line from your bow to the shore.

On the southern tip of St. Lucia is the fishing village of Vieux-Fort. On many of the Windward Islands you can buy fresh-ly caught fish, but you will probably also be approached by fisher-men who come to your boat. It's usually a very good deal to buy from these fishermen, and it's more fun than buying from a more traditional source. The islands also have a fruit indigenous to the region called a golden apple, sort of a cross between a peach and an apple, and one of the most delicious fruits I have ever tasted. We were told that golden apples don't "travel" well, so they are not exported, but personally I think they're so good the locals want to eat them all themselves.

St. Vincent

The next stop to the south is St. Vincent (Saint is pronounced "Sent"), the chief island in the country of St. Vincent and the Grenadines. St. Vincent is one of the most underrated islands in the world, a beautiful place with fabulous mountains and lush foliage. The botanical gardens in Kingstown are the oldest in the western hemisphere. The northern part of St. Vincent is dominated by Mount Soufriere which, along with Mount Pelée on Martinique, erupted at the turn of the century and killed many people. Mount Soufriere last erupted in the mid-1970s. If you are heading down from St. Lucia, you must go directly to Kingstown to clear customs.

Kingstown is a fun place with good restaurants, some featuring steel bands. The town also is a good place to provision, with a well-stocked supermarket. The buses into town are painted all colors of the rainbow, and each bus has its equally colorful name painted on it. You'll not only have locals on the bus, but probably their chickens as well. You'll need to take a taxi back if you buy provisions, since you won't be able to haul it all on a bus. The Kingstown outdoor market is great for fresh produce—and don't forget the golden apples. Visit the botanical gardens and then hike up to Fort Charlotte for a lovely view. The best place for anchoring at Kingstown is in Blue Lagoon off of Young Island, all of which lies in Callaqua Bay. Blue Lagoon is surrounded by reefs that provide a quiet anchorage. You can explore Young Island, which is a resort area with colorful birds placed around in cages.

Sailing up the western coast of St. Vincent (there are no anchorages on the eastern, or Atlantic, side), the first place you can stop for overnighting is Cumberland Bay. Anchor close to shore since the water is deep, except at the quay (where it is very shallow). Drop a stern anchor and tie a bow line ashore.

Continuing up the coast, head to Chateaubelair Island, go past the island, and sail east into Chateaubelair Bay. Anchor in the north to northwest part of the bay, again getting in fairly close to avoid putting down tons of anchor chain. You can arrange for a taxi to take you to where you can climb up Mount Soufriere.

From St. Vincent south to Grenada, the chain of islands known as the Grenadines is one of the finest sailing areas you will ever find. The area from St. Vincent to Petit St. Vincent is governed by St. Vincent. The area from Petit Martinique to Grenada is governed by the country of Grenada. Heading south, you can clear customs at Union Island.

From the southern tip of St. Vincent to the island of Bequia is a short sail, only about 6 miles, but it can be choppy; it's a seaway with Africa as the next stop east. There is a fairly strong westward-setting current. You can almost count on a school of dolphins leading partway across, doing their crisscross jumps in front of your bow and generally showing you that they belong there while we are merely given temporary license in their environment. Toward the southern portion of Bequia is a gigantic bay, Admiralty Bay, which is usually well filled with cruising and fishing boats. Approach from the west, avoiding Devil's Table to the north. Ashore in Port Elizabeth you can see wooden boats being built along the beach. The locally built boats vary somewhat from

Wooden boats built on Bequian beaches

island to island, but they are all a delight to look at. If you swim off the beach, it is not unusual to see large rays (they won't bother you) also enjoying a swim. Until just a few years ago, Bequians went whaling in open whale boats, using harpoons to catch their prey. The declining whale population in the area finally ended the practice. There is also an excellent model ship builder in Port Elizabeth who sells his models. The Frangipani Restaurant on the southern end of the beach has excellent food—don't miss the pumpkin soup—and is a lively nightspot around the bar and patio in the evening.

We had one unforgettable experience on Bequia that involved the local belief that if someone dies on the island, the wind will blow exceptionally hard—and the older the person was at the time of death, the stronger it will blow. The day we arrived, a 102-year-old lady had died—and our local friend Winfield expected a hurricane. We went the next day to the funeral, where the women were dressed in white with white veils, the men were dressed in black serge suits and wore derbies or fedoras, and the dignitaries wore red sashes. After the funeral we set sail in the normal fifteen- to eighteen-knot winds—which suddenly kicked up to forty-two knots. We all looked at one another and became believers.

Around the southern tip of Bequia is a fabulous sight, Moon Hole, a cave that goes through the island and in which houses now stand. You'll also see a house that looks like the bow of a boat coming out from the cliffs. At night you may well be serenaded by young locals who row around the anchored boats singing and playing guitars. Young children will also come out to sell you their coconut-shell boats, which actually sail quite well with their deep metal keels and miniature sails.

The islands between Bequia and Mustique are fine for gunkholing but do not provide any good anchorages. The island of Mustique is perhaps best known as one of Princess Margaret's retreats. About halfway down the western coast is Grand Bay. Stay well west of the island and approach the bay from the south to avoid Montezuma Shoal. On the way down you'll pass the wreck of a French cruise ship that went aground in the early 1970s. On the island, you may see what looks like a concrete road. It's actually an airstrip, and small planes land there, seeming to come from nowhere. From Mustique head south to the island of Cannouan. While there are anchorages around much of the island, the main harbor is Charlestown Bay at the southwestern end. There are numerous reefs, but the water is clear and the reefs easy to spot. Come in under power to control your progress, and anchor in the northeastern corner of the bay.

Your next stop is one of the highlights of the cruise and one I guarantee you'll never forget: the exotic Tobago Cays. You do have to be careful going in, and you should go in and out only under power. Come in from the northwest and leave the same way. Anchor between two of the cays, Petit Rameau and Petit Bateau. Sometimes local fishermen who camp on the beach are willing to sell freshly caught fish. A strong tide runs through here, so if you swim off the boat, put out a warp with a cushion tied to the end to allow you to grab hold if you find you're tiring. Take your dinghy over to Horse Shoe Reef, considered one of the best snorkeling areas in the world. The huge reef is populated with a wide variety of colorful fish that seem as fascinated by you as you are by them. You will also see many different types of coral. Words can't do justice to the beauty of the Tobago Cays. Go in your dinghy to all four cays, and take your snorkeling gear with you. It's something to behold waves from the Atlantic breaking outside Worlds End Reef as you swim in clear pools with fantastic coral and fish life around and beneath you.

After leaving the Tobago Cays from the northwest, sail west to Mayero. Salt Whistle Bay in the northwest corner of the island offers a pretty, well-protected anchorage with a crescent-shaped beach. Anchor close to shore. Farther south down the western shore of Mayero is Saline Bay, a good lunch stop but somewhat rolly for overnighting. If you will be leaving your boat in Grenada, skip Union Island for now since you will have to go over there to clear customs when heading south.

Sail over to Palm Island, a beautiful little resort island with a red-and-white salt-and-pepper beach that feels like talcum powder; it's crushed coral. Palm Island used to be called Prune Island, but for years a man named John Caldwell planted palm trees throughout the islands. In gratitude, the government gave him a 99-year lease on the island and permission to build a lovely little resort with cottages and a main building. The dining room is outside, with a thatched roof and walls extending up to table height. Impudent birds may fly in and steal food. Caldwell, a very personable fellow, is a well-known author and sailor and usually has time to spin some fascinating tales. Palm Island can be a pretty rolly overnight stop, since there is no real bay or cove to pull into.

Your next stop south is Petit St. Vincent, a beautiful island with a lovely resort that offers very sophisticated, well-appointed "cottages" from which guests can be picked up by cart to go to the restaurant. The food at the restaurant is excellent, and once a week they have a jump-up—a local dance well described by the name. The steel bands are fine, but the dancing is a little tame because it's mostly done by tourists (wait until you get to St. Georges in Grenada). You can also play Ping-Pong in the room just outside the dining area. On the eastern side of the island, fronting the Atlantic, is a very beautiful beach. Be careful as you take the path to the beach because you will pass a number of the poisonous manchineel trees, so be sure not to touch the fruit or stand under the trees. The first time I visited the beach, it was pristine, but on my last visit it was fouled with clumps of tar-like oil that had apparently been dumped from oil carriers.

Now head northwest over to Union Island, both to see the island and to clear out with customs. Union is a mystical-looking island, with its razorback mountains usually slicing into some

Petit St. Vincent

clouds. You can sail to the western side of the island to Chatham Bay for a lunch stop, then sail around to the eastern side to Clifton Bay to find the customs people. Clifton Bay has a large horseshoe reef, so come in slowly.

Grenada

Now drop down to Carriacou, a large island with restaurants, hotels, and mechanics who can help with recalcitrant diesels. Pull into Hillsboro to clear into customs (as in all customs clearing in these islands, you must present a crew list), then continue south to Tyrell Bay. Again, watch for coral reefs as you go in. The dock at Tyrell Bay is a hub of activity, particularly exciting when the ferry comes in to load and unload people, supplies, goats, and so forth. It was hilarious to see a cow being hoisted onto the dock (not, however, for the cow, who looked terrified). When you leave, gunkhole into Manchioneal Bay, then anchor off Saline Island for some good snorkeling.

Your next stop is Grenada. Stay west to avoid Diamond Island (locally known as Kick-em-Jenny due to occasional strong gusts in the area), Ronde Island, and the rocks known as The Sisters. There can be strong gusts blowing offshore along the western coast. We once took a blast off of Black Bay Point that really laid us over—but the nice thing about a forty-four-footer is the ballast, so it just gave us a momentary thrill. St. George's Harbor is nearly all the way to the southern end of the island. Just as you begin to fear you missed it, the harbor suddenly opens up to port, between the cliffs. There is an inner and outer harbor. The outer harbor is the Carenage, a lovely sheltered harbor with seawalls on three sides, shops and restaurants, and mostly commercial boats. The inner or southern harbor is the Lagoon, a perfect hurricane hole. You can tie up to a dock for a nominal fee, and you should plan to spend at least a couple of days here. You'll see fabulous boats with gleaming brightwork all around you and boatbuilding or repairing at the boatyard right across the Lagoon.

The people of Grenada are, next to the Thai, the friendliest I have met anywhere. Ask someone where the bakery is and, rather than just telling you, the person will walk 5 or 6 blocks out of the way to take you there. The food is great, especially conch (prepared in a variety of ways), just about any fish they have, and calaloo soup. Saturday evenings bring a jump-up that is not to be missed. This dance is not designed to entertain the tourists but is for the people who live here, and tourists may attend. The steel bands are great, the energy in the dancing is amazing, and the jump-up becomes a wonderful party with lots of laughing and friendly people. Grenada is a lush island well worth hiring a taxi and driver to help you tour. You'll drive up roads with hairpin turns, see women washing clothing in streams, look at a "lake" which is actually the mouth of a long-dormant volcano filled with water, and view trees, bushes, and flowers that will take your breath away.

United States Great Lakes

Whoever named these huge bodies of water "lakes" was a master of understatement. These are inland seas! The scenery in summer and fall is spectacular. From the end of May through the middle of October (when it can get pretty cool) is the best period to sail this area.

If you start from Harbor Springs in northern Michigan, you swing into Lake Michigan and head north to Mackinac Island, famous for the annual Mackinac Race and a popular area throughout the sailing season. Cars are not allowed on the island, but there are plenty of horse-drawn carriages for transportation. The state dock at Mackinac Island is usually crowded in the summer, less so in spring and fall. From Mackinac, head east into Lake Huron and anchor off of Drummond Island, with its lovely foliage. Just east, guarding the southern flank of the North Channel, is Canada's Manitoulin Island, almost one hundred miles long and the largest freshwater island in the world. At the western end of Manitoulin make a dogleg north and you head right into the North Channel. You're now in Canada.

Swing west and head over to Bruce Mines on the northern shore of the North Channel, where you'll find a marina that caters to transient boats. (The northern shoreline has what is considered the oldest rock on earth, said to be about three billion years old.) Then head east to Long Point Cove to a quiet anchorage surrounded by rock walls. Across the North Channel, on Manitoulin

The schooner *Manitou*, one of the largest sailing vessels on the Great Lakes *(Traverse Tall Ship Co.)*

Island, is Gore Bay, where a small village offers stores and restaurants. Staying on the Manitoulin side of the channel, continue east to Little Current and tie up to the dock.

Little Current, on the northeast end of Manitoulin, is sort of the hub of the North Channel and provides excellent provisioning. From here, go north to the Benjamin Islands, North and South. These uninhabited islands offer excellent hiking and, during season, very tasty blueberries. Farther east on the northern shore of the channel is Bay Finn, a fjord bounded by majestic cliffs and ending in a lake-like anchorage—The Pool—that provides perfect shelter from any direction. Staying on the northern shore, sail east to the pretty anchorage at Portage Couvert. Just east of here is Killarney, a town where you can buy provisions and hike on various trails. The water all through here is crystal clear.

The Six Most Unusual Areas To Charter

The areas we will discuss here are ones that don't get a lot of publicity about their cruising appeal and are seldom considered by charterers from the U.S.—even though they are delightful cruising grounds. Yes, they're unusual, and yes, they're worth considering as you choose places to cruise.

Corsica and Sardinia

West of Italy are the fascinating islands of Corsica, which is French, and Sardinia, which is Italian. These islands are bounded by three different seas: the Ligurian to the north, the Tyrrhenian to the east, and the Mediterranean to the south and west. Close to each other geographically, the islands are as different in character as France is from Italy. The sailing in Corsica and Sardinia is easy, the island scenery lovely, and the food outstanding, although a little bit more expensive than in other Mediterranean areas such as Greece or Turkey. May through September is the best time for chartering. Nights can be cool.

Corsica

Corsica, Napoleon's birthplace, is the northernmost of the two islands. The cooking, while French, is prepared Corsican style; if you like bouillabaisse, Corsica is the place to have it. A good place to begin a Corsican cruise is halfway up the eastern coast at Solenzara—a town with a few small restaurants, a marina, and a swimming beach—where you can provision. Sail south from here to the Gulf of Porto Vecchio. You can gunkhole into a number of smaller coves and beaches, but none are suitable for overnight anchoring until Porto Vecchio. The harbor is surrounded on the south, west, and north by mountains. It's worthwhile to hire a car and drive up into the mountains to see the lovely scenery. The town itself is a fascinating old, walled village.

Sailing farther down the coast, you will reach the large, well-sheltered anchorage at Port de Rondinara. The swimming is excellent in very clear water. Continue your cruise south and around the base of Corsica, then about 5 miles up the western coast to Bonifacio. The fjord-like harbor, offering wonderful protection, is dominated by a fort that is a base for the French Foreign Legion. A number of good restaurants share the quay; for breakfast be sure to get steaming hot bread and croissants from the bakery. Sail next to the Lavezzi Islands, just off the southeast coast of Corsica, for a lunch stop, your last in Corsican waters. Except for a lighthouse keeper, these islands are uninhabited. The water is clear, right down to the sandy bottom.

Sardinia

Staying on a southeast course from the Lavezzi Islands, you will come into Sardinian waters, arriving first at the Maddalena Islands. This is a small archipelago with numerous coves and nice beaches good for snorkeling. Stop off at Santa Maria for lunch, then head down to Spargi for the night. Next day make a lunch stop at San Stefano, then stop over at Caprera.

Your first stop on the Sardinian mainland is at the northeast corner, at Palau, about a 5-mile sail. Have lunch there; the clams are top-notch. Continue southeast to Porto Cervo, a major tourist area catering to the well-to-do, with a spectacular harbor financed by the Aga Khan. Just south of the harbor is the old and busy town of Olbia, where you will find some fine restaurants. Next day you can take a nice sail down the east coast to Cagliari Harbor on the southeast corner of Sardinia.

The Norfolk Broads

On the southeastern side of Great Britain are the Norfolk Broads. "Broads" is another word for lakes; there are over forty of them, all connected by rivers and canals. The Broads provide a very unusual type of cruising. The area is pastoral and quiet, with a lot of bird life and with villages that appear not to have changed in a couple of hundred years. The best time to visit is late May through mid-September. You can spend anywhere from four days to two weeks or more cruising the Broads.

Special sailboats have been designed for these waters. Broads boats are shallow-draft vessels ranging in length from twenty-five to thirty feet, with beams of eight to ten feet. They are gaff-rigged sloops with centerboards to accommodate the shallow water. In cruising the Broads, you'll encounter numerous bridges—none of which raise or swivel—so the masts on these boats have been cleverly designed to pivot on a tabernacle aided by a counter-weight and controlled by a tackle attached to the forestay. In a short time you will get the hang of it and will be able to sail up to a bridge, lower the mast, motor under the bridge, and quickly get the rig back up on the other side. There are close to 150 miles of inland waterways in the Broads, many lined with windmills long gone into disuse. Some areas have thick pockets of tall reeds, giv-ing you the feeling that you're sailing on land. Along the way are a number of nature preserves and many opportunities for taking hikes. You'll also see something reminiscent of the Orient—the Broads Floating Food Market, from which you can purchase sup-plies. I imagine there is a schedule for this market, but I never did determine it. The market just seemed to pop up in various places and was always a welcome sight.

As long as you don't block traffic, you can anchor just about wherever you wish along the river banks (excluding areas that are obviously private). This gives you a great deal of flexibility in your travels. Many small villages have docks or quays, but they tend to be small and on a first-come, first-served basis, so unless you stop early you will probably have to anchor.

You can start your trip through the Broads at Wroxham, in the northwest section, and then proceed in a serpentine but basically east-southeast direction down the River Bure. The next town is on a northeast leg of the "serpent." This is Horning, a very pleasant vil-lage to walk around. As you sail farther east-southeast, you will reach the point where the Bure joins the rivers Ant and Thurne. Anchor and go ashore to visit St. Benet's Abbey. Then head up the Ant to Ludham and go ashore to see the pretty little village.

After Ludham, return to the Bure and travel up the River Thurne to Potter Heigham and the lovely bridge spanning the river at this point. Enjoy a meal at the Bridge Inn. Then go all the way up to Hickling Broad. The pub at Hickling Staithe caters to the boating trade and serves excellent food. Come back down to the Thurne and visit Acle, where you will find good eating at the Acle Bridge.

Ireland

Along with being picturesque, the southern coast of Ireland seems to always have wind—very nice if you're on a sailboat. This is one sailing area, however, where you should definitely pack your foul-weather gear, because the weather can be quite variable. You may not need a swimsuit unless you're used to swimming in Maine on its one day of summer; the water is cold. But don't let the climate deter you. Southern Ireland is great for cruising, and the people are exceptionally friendly, with the inhabitants of the pubs treating you like an old friend. The best time of year for sailing is from the end of May to mid-September. Evenings can get quite cool, in the low sixties or high fifties.

Several ports have marinas, and many harbors offer good protected anchoring. The tides run over twelve feet, so don't drop your hook in a shallow area at high tide or you'll be stuck when the tide turns. The tide is strong and has a tendency to push you toward shore. This is nothing to be alarmed about, but you should

Rossbrin anchorage, Ireland (*Rossbrin Yacht Charters*)

take the tide into account so you won't have to buck its effect.

You can provision in Cork, a large city built on two hills, where you will find good restaurants and nightlife—and a deep, well-protected harbor. As you sail out, head over to the southeast corner of the harbor to Cobh and visit the beautiful cathedral there. Across from Cobh is Spike Island, formerly a prison island. Sail northeast and swing west into Ballycotton Bay for a visit, and then continue on to Youghal Bay and the town of Youghal, which was a major Irish port in the 1400s. The tides are strong, so it's a good idea to drop a kedge as well as the main anchor. You'll find good pubs and restaurants in Youghal.

Next day head southwest for a nice sail to Crosshaven at the entrance to Cork Bay. This village boasts the oldest yacht club in the world, established in the early 1700s. The following day swing farther southwest into the fascinating village of Kinsale. Charles Fort, high overhead at the harbor entrance, is open for sightseeing. The restaurants in Kinsale are good, especially the Bistro. Continue southwest, pulling into Courtmacsherry Bay for a look-see, then sail past the Seven Heads and into Clonakilty Bay for a lunch stop. Clear Island, off Ireland's southern tip, makes a good overnight stop. There are two small harbors, but the one to the north provides the best protection. You'll be ringed by steep cliffs, with crystal-clear water down to the sandy bottom.

On the following day, sail west. Off to port you'll see the famous Fastnet Rock poking up, namesake for the Fastnet Race and the site where the 1979 race turned into disaster as many boats were abandoned and sunk because of high winds and bad weather conditions that struck unexpectedly. (These conditions are most likely to occur in fall and winter, when there is no chartering in the area.) Just after Mizen Head, swing southwest and head into Dunmanus Bay for lunch, then go farther up the coast to Bantry Bay, a large, long bay. Head all the way up to the northwest corner of the bay at Glengariff, where a very narrow entrance opens into a harbor ringed by mountains and pine-covered hills.

Great Slave Lake

Only 400 miles south of the Arctic Circle, Great Slave Lake offers twenty-four hours of daylight in the summer. Here is the northernmost charter company in the world. Great Slave Lake in the Northwest Territories of Canada is the third largest freshwater lake in North America, with water pure enough to drink and ice for the ice chest available by just chipping it off. Once you provision, you are on your own; there are no restaurants or help available once you leave Yellowknife. The fishing is great, the chances are you will see moose, and if you're there in August or September you can see the Northern Lights. The long hours of northern daylight mean there is no restriction on sailing at night, so only your internal clock governs your schedule. After a few days you will find yourself sailing at two or three in the morning and, except when you look at your watch, it doesn't seem strange at all.

Chartering on the Great Slave occurs from late June through early September. Temperatures can go into the eighties during the day but drop into the fifties at night. For all but the most hardy, the water is too cold for swimming except perhaps in some shallow areas not sheltered by trees. The Great Slave offers a type of cruise very different from the more typical cruise, for sailors who are self-sufficient. It's a charter you will always remember.

Yellowknife, on the northwest edge of the lake, is a good-size city with restaurants, hotels, shops of every kind, and supermarkets for provisioning. You have to keep an eye out for both shallows and reefs in the northern section of the lake; use your depth finder since the charts are not reliable, providing only approximate information. Head down Yellowknife Channel, turn south past Detah, and pull into Drybones Bay for a good overnight anchorage. This is a nice long sail of about 30 miles. The name Drybones comes from the local Indian practice of leaving the dead on rocks to dry out, and then covering the bones with rocks. Drybones Bay is a good place to spot moose.

Continue southeast to Devil's Channel, a long narrow waterway leading to the East Arm. (One bay in the area is called Danforth Bay because a hapless sailor threw out his Danforth anchor without first attaching it to an anchor line. Many of the bays are unnamed, at least on the charts.) Toward the eastern end of Devil's Channel you can see a native burial ground. Farther on is a small, very pretty anchorage, Lady Jane Bay.

Continue your cruise by sailing east for about 20 miles to the cove at Hole-in-the-Wall, with cliffs 250 to 300 feet high and a

A long-awaited reward (*Whitsunday Rent A Yacht*)

geologic history dating back millions of years. It's a nice hike to the top of the cliffs, affording a lovely view across Hearne Channel. Next day swing northeast to Christopher's Pocket. There are numerous islands and anchorages all along the East Arm. Two safe and pretty overnight stops are at the opposite ends of Blanchet Island: Nipin Bay on the eastern end and Shelter Bay at the western end.

Australia

Some of the best sailors in the world come from Australia, but it's unusual to find Americans sailing its waters. The well-publicized friendliness of the Australians is not exaggerated, and their informality seems to make you a friend almost immediately.

Off the North Queensland coast of Australia lie seventy-four magical and mostly uninhabited islands, the Whitsundays, along with the Great Barrier Reef to the east. The sailing here can be dangerous due to coral and shifting sandbars, so you can bareboat, with restrictions placed by the charter operator on the area you can cruise, or go crewed bareboat and see it all. The charter fleets are all based at Queensland's Arlie Beach.

An Australian cruise offers isolated beaches, excellent fishing and snorkeling, and for the plusher life, major resort areas on Hamilton and Hayman islands. The variety of fish life is extraordinary, and on some of the islands you'll find black-faced goats with blue eyes, descendants left behind by seamen who originally explored these islands and left the animals so that people who followed would find food.

The Great Barrier Reef, formed by coral, is the largest living thing on earth, and offers fabulous diving, snorkeling, and swimming. The beaches, in all sizes, are truly isolated, giving you the feeling of being on your own private beach. The best period for a cruise in the Whitsundays is from late October to early May (remember that you're in the southern hemisphere), since the winds can get pretty strong in the winter months.

North Carolina

One area that doesn't get the chartering activity it deserves is North Carolina's Pamlico Sound and the Outer Banks. The Sound is quite shallow, rarely beyond 20 feet and frequently far less than that, while the tributary rivers tend to be fairly deep and navigable. For the best winds and to avoid the heat of midsummer, sail this area from May through the middle of July or from mid-September through October.

You can start a cruise near the head of the Pamlico River at the town of Washington, also known as Little Washington. As you near the bridge there, turn to power because you'll have to wait until the bridge is opened. Then tie up to the town dock; it's free. Many of the municipal docks in the area are free and also supply water at no charge. The town itself is nice to walk around.

Heading southeast, sail into Broad Creek and continue on down to Bath Creek and the town of Bath. The town has a nice harbor, a pretty little beach, and the oldest church in North Carolina (dating back to the 1730s). Take a walk around town and visit the red brick house that belonged to the pirate Blackbeard (Edward Teach). The house was his haven between "business trips." Next day continue east-southeast until you reach the Pungo River to port and head up to Belhaven. It's a lovely sail up the river, and Belhaven is a pleasant town for strolling.

Come back down the river the next morning and gunkhole around Cedar Island, and then head west to Oriental on the north shore of the Neuse River. Oriental claims to be the sailing capital of North Carolina, with more than a thousand sailboats calling it home, and it is an excellent overnight stop. From Oriental, ease back into the Neuse River and sail south into Adams Creek, which turns into Core Creek and then the Newport River. At the end of the river, turn to port to Beaufort. Beaufort is a pretty town with many houses dating back to the 1600s and 1700s. The maritime museum there is worth a visit. Spend some time that evening at Dockside, a fun place right on the dock. The hot dogs at the Royal James are particularly good.

One highlight of cruising this area lies about 20 miles to the east. This is Ocracoke Island, a narrow 16-mile-long finger that is part of the Outer Banks. Except for Ocracoke Village, the island is a national park, with sand dunes and salt marshes on the Pamlico Sound side and beaches along the Atlantic Ocean side. Talk to your charterer about current conditions. Sandbanks constantly change here, although maritime authorities do a pretty good job of keeping on top of this and marking the navigable channels. At the southwestern end of Ocracoke is Silver Lake, a good overnight stop. Of the two entrances, Big Foot Channel is your safest choice. You can either anchor here or tie up to the dock, which is free. You'll find excellent food at a number of restaurants in Silver Lake, particularly the Back Porch. All the fish and shellfish dishes here are delicious, but you have to try the Cayenne deviled crab.

Ocracoke Island was Blackbeard's major base of operations and you'll hear stories about him from many of the residents. The lighthouse on Ocracoke is the second oldest still in use in the United States. Farther out, wild ponies still range the dunes. The ponies are said to be the descendants either of horses brought over during Spanish exploration or of horses that survived shipwrecks 200 to 300 years ago. You'll also find a small cemetery with the graves of four British sailors who were killed just offshore during World War II by a German U-boat. Numerous hiking trails are well-maintained by the National Park Service. Ocracoke was primarily settled by survivors of shipwrecks back when this Cape Hatteras area earned its name of Graveyard of the Atlantic. While some tourist trade has sprung up, Ocracoke is still basically a fishing village.

The Five Most Challenging Areas to Charter—and Reasons to Try Them

The areas we will visit in this chapter offer fantastic sailing and scenery and, in many instances, little boat traffic. For any of a number of reasons, however, such as difficult weather, strong wind and tides, reefs, or rocks, these are areas that should be sailed only by experienced cruisers with adequate crew.

Scotland

We'll start with the wild and woolly west coast of Scotland between the fifty-sixth and fifty-seventh parallels. First the bad news: you can expect variable weather with strong winds and tides and perhaps fog, limiting chartering to only May through mid June. About the warmest it will get is seventy degrees, and it may well drop down into the high forties. Except for a few harbors, you're on your own. You must be flexible in your itinerary since the weather and wind conditions can change so suddenly. Now the good news: the sailing is terrific, and the rugged scenery is spectacular, including the occasional profile of a castle backlit against the sky. This is one cruise in which the aura of the place is an especially integral part of the experience.

Let's start our cruise from Craobh Haven, northeast of Jura Island and east of Luing Island. Head southwest and then swing northwest at the southern tip of Luing, skirt Fadda, and sail across the Firth of Lorne to Loch Buie, the deep bay on the southeast coast of the Isle of Mull. The isle provides a shield from heavy wind and is a wonderful place to explore. Now head back to the Firth of Lorne, sail up the east coast of Mull, and pull in through the narrow entrance to the wide bay just southwest of Kerrera, Loch Spelve, for an overnight stay. The large castle high up on the

Off the west coast of Scotland *(Skyes'l Charters)*

cliff at the eastern tip of the bay is Duart Castle and dates back to the 1200s.

The Sound of Mull, a body of water extending northwest and southeast from the eastern edge of the Isle of Mull, affords good protection under most wind and weather conditions. Swing to starboard for a visit to Ardtornish Bay on the Morvern Peninsula, and drop the hook just below the remains of the castle there. This is a lunch stop, not a good place for overnighting. Now head up the Sound of Mull to the northeastern tip of the Isle of Mull, and pull into Tobermory, an excellent anchorage. You can dinghy ashore to eat at the Mishnish Hotel and to visit the famous Tobermory Distillery, where you can stock up on some liquid warmth. East across the Sound, on the Morvern Peninsula, is Loch Na Droma Buidhe, another very good anchorage. Head into the deep cut on the Movern side and then swing southeast into the loch.

If you hit a very mild spell with forecasts of continued good weather, you can sail down the western coast of Mull and see some exciting scenery on the small islands of Treshnish, Gometra, and Staffa. You may be able to anchor east of Treshnish in Loch Tuath if the wind direction is not westerly. Staffa is the site of Fingal's Cave, which is easily visible as you sail by. At the western tip of the Ross of Mull, an arm of land extending west of Mull, is Iona Island. If you head east on the northern shore of the Ross of Mull, you can pull into Loch Scridain and the town of Bunessan. Continue east back into the Firth of Lorne to the island of Kerrera, just opposite Oban on the mainland. Then go to Oban, a nice town to roam and also to provision. The chances are that you will wear your foul-weather gear for at least part of the time during your Scotland cruise, but the combination of great sailing and rugged scenery will be worth it.

Nova Scotia

From Scotland let's head to .New Scotland, otherwise known as Nova Scotia, one of Canada's Maritime Provinces. Nova Scotia boasts some good-size cities with all amenities. For the most part, however, Nova Scotia offers a series of small fishing villages that appear not to have changed much over time. Tranquil and picturesque, many are favorite haunts of artists who come to paint the wonderful maritime views. June through August is the best period to charter with daytime temperatures ranging from about fifty degrees to near eighty. It's cool at night even in early August. Nova Scotia provides the opportunity to cruise an area that is devoted to maritime industries and is still almost totally unspoiled.

The huge, deep Bay of Fundy separates New Brunswick and Nova Scotia. The Bay of Fundy has the highest tides in the world, fifty feet—yes, a fifty-foot rise and fall. You won't believe your eyes when you see what looks like a great sailing or swimming area disappear and turn into red mud as the tide turns on the Bay of Fundy. You can also count on dense fog, which burns off around ten o'clock most summer mornings. The harbors and scenery, especially for anyone who loves boating, are unsurpassed. The tides and fog, however, dictate more than novice experience in sailing.

You can start from Halifax, where you can easily provision, find loads of excellent restaurants and shops, visit a wonderful maritime museum, and see a replica of the famous racing schooner *Bluenose*. Halifax is a busy international port. There are a number of good harbors on this southern coast, most fairly close to one another. Sail first to the southwestern tip of the peninsula that extends southwest of Halifax to Peggy's Cove (a moonscape-looking harbor because of all its rugged rocks). On shore is a small, pretty park.

Continue southwest down the coast to Mahone Bay, with its three churches alongside each other at the head of the bay. You can buy meals at just about all of Nova Scotia's villages. We were disappointed on one trip, however, to find that by the beginning of August, nearly all the lobsters had been shipped down to the United States. Our salivary glands were kept in constant motion due to the thousands of lobster traps that are seen in virtually every village. Mahone Bay is a craft center and hosts a Wooden Boat Festival every August. A short distance southwest is Lunenburg, a major fishing port and fast becoming a major tourist area. Lunenburg, with both an inner and outer harbor, offers everything from restaurants, banks, shopping, and museums to boat repair facilities. Every September the town has the Nova Scotia Fisheries Exhibition and Fisherman's Reunion, highlighted by dory racing. Lunenburg was the home of the *Bluenose* and is the official home of *Bluenose II*. Sail over to Blue Rocks and the fantastic ledges there, and take a look at the cave known as the Ovens.

There are many other lovely coves and harbors along the Nova Scotia coast, especially near the southeastern tip at the village of Shelburne. This town, settled during the American Revolution by British loyalists, has a few interesting museums. At the Dory Shop, wooden dories are still built.

On the southern tip of Nova Scotia is the fishing town of Clark's Harbour, with an active fish plant and boat-building yards. Going up what is known as the northern coast of Nova Scotia, you will reach Wedgeport, a town settled in the late 1700s and a major fishing area for herring and mackerel. A little farther up the coast is the major port of Yarmouth. The Yarmouth County Museum displays a fabulous collection of ship paintings and the Runic Stone, one of the testimonials to Norse exploration of the area.

There is a way to sail in Nova Scotia without worrying about the tides or fog. This alternative is offered by the huge Bras d'Or Lakes, at the northeastern end of Nova Scotia in the middle of Cape Breton Island. The tide rises and falls only a few feet, there is rarely any fog, and this inland sea offers numerous attractive coves and bays. The friendly town of Baddeck on the lake has a marina, many nice restaurants, and the Alexander Graham Bell Museum. You can buy some nice Scotch woolen goods in Baddeck. The

Cruising Maine's rugged coast (*Morris Yacht Charters*)

Bras d'Or Yacht Club holds an annual regatta around early August, and the Cruising Club of America originated here.

Maine

In the islands of Maine, you have to watch out for rock ledges, but the primary hazard is fog. If your navigational skills are sufficient, this is one great area to cruise. Many of the islands are uninhabited, and those with people remain in much their original state, with just a house or cottage to break up the pristine view. The Maine coast of the United States and its coastal islands offer rugged scenery and spectacular sailing. The water is usually too cold for swimming. The best months for chartering are July and August, when daytime temperatures are in the high seventies to low eighties. It can drop into the fifties at night.

We'll start with Penobscot Bay. Leaving from Bass Harbor, head southwest. Be sure to skirt Weaver's Ledge, and then sail past Lopaus Point and up the western coast of Mt. Desert Island to the bay well described by its name, Pretty Marsh. Anchor in either of the two coves just past Folly Island. Next day head up Blue Hill Bay up the eastern side of Long Island. At the northern tip of Long Island, head south and then west into Eggemoggin Reach to Harbor Island and Bucks Harbor. The best anchorage is on the northeast side of the harbor. There is a good restaurant here. Sail west the following day to the mainland and Camden, a busy town with many good restaurants and stores. Camden is a good place for provisioning. Just around the little peninsula jutting out to the south is Rockport, a good place to buy shoes—and a good overnight stop.

Continue your cruise the next day by sailing south around Owls Head and then north to gunkhole around Islesboro Island and the harbor at Castine. On the following day, head south of Rockport to the pretty and secure bay at Pulpit Harbor. Sail south again the next day to the Muscle Ridge Islands (about a dozen in total), and keep an eye on your chart and your depth; the water gets pretty shallow here. Most of the islands are privately owned. The tidal range in this area is about ten feet. Head north to North Haven Island for overnighting and reprovisioning, if needed. For the next day's sail, head in the Fox Island Thorofare, just south of

North Haven, and sail among the small islands south of Deer Isle. Anchorages abound. Continue east the following day to Sand Cove on Marshall Island for a lunch stop, and then sail northeast to Burnt Coal Harbor on Swans Island. From Swans, head north to the pretty harbor of Frenchboro on the southern side of Long Island.

An alternative cruise is in Casco Bay, where the Maine Island Trail Association has established access to a 300-mile-long archipelago of islands. Some are private and some are state owned. The association has arranged for permission for cruisers to land on these islands and, in some cases, to camp overnight, providing that everything is left exactly as it was found. You could spend an enjoyable month or more in these islands alone.

New Zealand

New Zealand and the Tasman Sea have some of the strongest seas and winds in the world. They also have some of the best sailing. The Bay of Islands on the northeast corner of New Zealand's North Island seems to get most of the publicity and is admittedly a wonderful place to sail. But South Island offers Marlborough Sound. The sound, just west of Cook Strait and its notorious 150-knot winds, can get very gusty and therefore requires some sailing experience—but what a great place to sail.

The Marlborough Sound area has been established as a maritime park, which helps to keep it undeveloped. As you leave Picton to cruise up Queen Charlotte Sound, you'll notice that the water shelves steeply to about sixteen fathoms. Head into Camp Bay for an overnight stop. You can continue your cruise by heading farther west to Motueka. On the following day, you can swing north and then west into the large bay at Collingwood. You can sail for days and days around the sound, gunkholing into coves and bays and encountering very little boat traffic. The scenery is terrific, and the sailing boisterous. December through April is the prime sailing season.

Fiji Islands

The archipelago of the Fiji Islands, about 900 nautical miles north of New Zealand, is a land of enchantment. Unlike many of the

South Pacific islands, only a few of the Fijian islands have suc-
cumbed to the race toward modernization. The archipelago of
more than 300 islands has changed principally in the fact that
cannibalism is no longer practiced (these islands used to be called
the Cannibal Isles). The area around the Fijis is prone to rough
storms and dotted with barrier reefs. These factors, coupled with
the fact that only inaccurate charts are available, limit chartering
to crewed bareboats, since no charter operator is willing to risk
his boats.

Your hired skipper will not only know his way around the
waters and be familiar with local weather conditions, but will also
function as a knowledgeable tour guide. The skipper can explain
what you'll be seeing and tell you how to adhere to local customs
(which are very different from what you are used to). Some exam-
ples: When you reach an island, the first thing to do is to meet the
local chieftain; the greeting is a handshake and a smile. Take off
your shoes before entering a house. If you are offered a drink of
kava, made from a native root, drink it (preferably in one gulp);
the kava may taste like dishwater, but refusal to drink it is
extremely impolite. It is also impolite to refuse a gift. And it is
considered impolite to tip because Fijians feel that service is freely
given. When talking to someone it is considered good manners to
cross your arms and look the other person in the eye.

Fiji's main island is Vita Levu, and tourism has gained a
foothold here. Once you leave Vita Levu, the atmosphere becomes
increasingly relaxed. You will probably provision on Vanua Levu
at SavuSavu, a village with only a single street. Your skipper will
help you decide what to see and do in the islands. The snorkeling
is just great, and you can visit fabulous beaches, plantations, small
local villages, and isolated islands. You probably would not be
able to get to more than a fraction of Fiji's good areas without
someone who knows these waters well. If you catch any fish, be
sure to show them to the skipper, because some of the fish are
poisonous if eaten. Surprisingly, the same type of fish that is edi-
ble in one area can be poisonous in another.

May through November is the period to charter, avoiding the
cyclone season. May and October can be hot, well up in the
nineties, while June through September is 10 to 15 degrees cooler. Evenings can be cool enough to wear a sweater.

Part Three:
Worldwide Directory
of Charter Operators

About the Directory

This directory is organized by region, listing charter operators servicing each area. We have provided as much detailed information as was available. Where information is lacking (indicated as "not available"), it either was not provided by the charterer or could not be found among the company literature. Contact the charter operator for more information.

Charter operators that service more than one area are listed under each region they service. The number of boats kept by such operators in a particular region may vary because an operator may ferry some boats from one area to another depending upon season or demand. Some charter companies are not listed at all because they provided no information or because the data they sent was too general to allow placing them geographically.

Listing of a charterer is not meant to be an endorsement. We advise that you carefully check out a charter organization before making firm arrangements with that company.

The Cost of Chartering

Your cost for chartering a boat depends on many variables: location, size of the boat, type of charter, time of year, number of people, optional side trips, who provisions the boat, and whether airfare is included. A two-week charter is common. In the past few years, the cost for two-week charters I have taken has ranged from $480 to $3,500, excluding onshore eating and the purchasing of gifts.

With such a wide cost differential, there is a charter for virtually every budget. And, if you consider chartering as an alternative to staying at a hotel, the daily cost compares very favorably, plus you have the benefit of taking your "hotel" to various places without having to unpack and tote luggage. Also, shoreside dinners can be a bargain. In many areas (Greece, Turkey, Thailand, etc.) top-notch quality meals can be had for $3 including a beer and the tip.

Let's look at the variables I mentioned above. Location influences price in several ways. Some locations are more costly than others because the operator's expenses in maintaining a fleet in the area are high. Some charter costs are high simply because there is little competition in an area. Your cost of getting to the site must be figured in. If you live on the east coast of the United States, it will of course cost a lot less to get to Maine, Florida, or the Bahamas than to fly to Australia. (But if you can afford it, what a treat to sail in Australia!)

Naturally the cost of the boat increases with the size; no one would expect to pay the same amount for a 28-footer as they would for a 44-foot boat. The length of time you charter, of course, also affects cost.

The type of charter influences the price. A flotilla charter costs more than straight bareboating. A crewed charter costs even more, because the crew's time must be paid for. You will probably also find variation in costs from one charter organization to another in the same area, although it generally will not be major. Keep in mind that charter companies change prices from time to time, so don't assume that costs from several years back have remained the same. The time of year also affects cost since many areas have high and low seasons, with the high season being the time that demand for boats is at its peak.

The number of people sharing your charter affects your individual cost. If five people rent a thirty-five-footer for $2,000 for the two weeks, the cost comes to $400 per person. But reduce the crew to four, and the cost per person jumps to $500. You may have the choice of provisioning the boat yourself or paying the charter company to do it. It usually costs more to have the company handle the provisioning, but the cost may well be worth the convenience to you. Some charter operators offer side trips, which bring added cost. Airfare sometimes is included in the total package—but it's usually not. The charter operator, however, may be able to arrange favorable flights and fares for you.

Carefully check out your potential charter operator, and compare that operator's costs with other charterers who have similar facilities and reputation. Your budget may preclude a cruise to

Thailand (which would be a shame), but sailing Lake Huron or the Florida Keys or the San Juan Islands can still provide an unforgettable vacation. Or you may economize by a one-week or partial-week charter rather than a two-week cruise. By working at it, you will be able to find a charter that will not only be affordable, but will provide you with memories that last a lifetime.

United States West Coast, Alaska, and Canada

ABC Yacht Charters
Cruising area: San Juan and Gulf islands, Desolation Sound
Types of charters: Bareboat, crewed
Boat length: 31 to 50 feet
Number of boats: Not available
High season: June 13–September 25
Low season: September 26–June 12
Mailing address: 1905 Skyline Way, Anacortes, WA 98221
Telephone: (800) 426–2313 or (206) 293–9533
Fax: (206) 293–0313

Adventure Charters
Cruising area: San Juan and Gulf islands
Types of charters: Crewed
Boat length: 45 feet
Number of boats: 1
High season: July 1–September 30
Low season: April 1–June 30 and October 1–October 30
Mailing address: P.O. Box 4314, Friday Harbor, WA 98250
Telephone: Not available

Alaskan Wilderness Sailing Safaris
Cruising area: Prince William Sound, Alaska
Types of charters: Crewed, flotilla
Boat length: 27 to 40 feet
Number of boats: 4
High season and low season: May 29–September 12
Mailing address: P.O. Box 1313, Valdez, AK 99686
Telephone: (907) 835–5175
Fax: (907) 835–3765

Anacortes Yacht Charters

Cruising area: San Juan Islands north to Alaska
Types of charters: Bareboat, crewed, flotilla
Boat length: 27 to 46 feet
Number of boats: 90
High season: July 1–September 30
Low season: October 1–May 31
Mailing address: P.O. Box 69, Anacortes, WA 98221
Telephone: (800) 233–3004 or (206) 293–4555

Bellhaven Charters

Cruising area: San Juan and Gulf islands
Types of charters: Bareboat, crewed
Boat length: 28 to 43 feet
Number of boats: Not available
High season: June 20–September 4
Low season: May 30–June 19 and September 5–September 25
Mailing address: #9 Squalicum Mall, Bellingham, WA 98225
Telephone: (800) 542–8812 or (206) 733–6636
Fax: (206) 647–9664

Bosun's Charters Ltd.

Cruising area: San Juan and Gulf islands
Types of charters: Bareboat, crewed, flotilla
Boat length: 29 to 40 feet
Number of boats: 20
High season: June 27–September 11
Low season: April 25–June 26 and September 12–September 27
Mailing address: P.O. Box 2464, Sydney, B.C., V8L 3Y3 Canada
Telephone: (604) 656–6644
Fax: (604) 656–4935

CA Charter Associates, Inc.

Cruising area: San Juan and Gulf islands, Desolation Bay
Types of charters: Bareboat, crewed, sailing school
Boat length: 30 to 44 feet
Number of boats: 20
High season: June 30–September 7
Low season: September 8–June 29
Mailing address: Box 1864, Point Roberts, WA 98281

Telephone: (604) 872–7210
Fax: (604) 873–9055

Cass' Marina, Inc.
Cruising area: San Francisco Bay
Types of charters: Bareboat, crewed, sailing/cruising school
Boat length: 22 to 55 feet
Number of boats: Not available
High season: Not available
Low season: Not available
Mailing address: 1702 Bridgeway at Napa Street, P.O. Box 643, Sausalito, CA 94900
Telephone: (415) 332–6789

Clipper Sailing Charters
Cruising area: San Juan and Gulf islands, Puget Sound
Types of charters: Crewed
Boat length: 53 feet
Number of boats: 1
High season: June 1–August 1
Low season: Not available
Mailing address: 7410 West Twenty-fifth Street, Tacoma, WA 98466
Telephone: (206) 565–5246

Club Nautique
Cruising area: San Francisco
Types of charters: Bareboat, crewed, flotilla, sailing/cruising school
Boat length: 23 to 45 feet
Number of boats: 47
High season: March 15–November 15
Low season: November 15–March 15
Mailing address: 1150 Ballena Boulevard, Suite 161, Alameda, CA 94501
Telephone: (415) 865–4700

Cooper Boating Center
Cruising area: San Juan and Gulf islands, Desolation Sound, British Columbia
Types of charters: Bareboat, crewed, flotilla

Puget Sound offers excellent sailing *(Clipper Sailing Charters)*

Boat length: 33 to 45 feet
Number of boats: 40
High season: June 27–September 7
Low season: April 17–June 26 and September 8–October 12
Mailing address: 1620 Duranleau Street, Granville Island,
   Vancouver, B.C., V6H 3S4 Canada
Telephone: (604) 687–4110

Dana Harbor Yacht Charters

Cruising area: California to Point Conception
Types of charters: Bareboat, crewed, sailing school
Boat length: 30 to 42 feet
Number of boats: 12
High season: May 1–September 30
Low season: October 1–April 30
Mailing address: 34571 Golden Lantern, Dana Point, CA 92629
Telephone: (714) 493–1206

D'Anna Yacht Center, Inc.

Cruising area: San Francisco Bay
Types of charters: Bareboat, crewed
Boat length: 24 to 31 feet
Number of boats: 10
High season: April 1–November 15
Low season: November 16–March 31
Mailing address: 11 Embarcadero West, #100, Oakland, CA 94607
Telephone: (800) 262–5959 or (510) 451–7000

Desolation Sound Yacht Charters Ltd.

Cruising area: Desolation Sound, Puget Sound
Types of charters: Bareboat, skippered
Boat length: 27 to 45 feet
Number of boats: 35
High season: July 5–August 29
Low season: May 1–July 4 and August 30–September 30
Mailing address: 201-1797 Comox Avenue, Comox, B.C., V9N
   4A1 Canada
Telephone: (604) 339–7222
Fax: (604) 339–2217

Duen Sailing Adventures, Inc.
Cruising area: From Northwest Washington state to Alaska
Types of charters: Crewed
Boat length: 72 feet
Number of boats: 1
High season: June 1–August 31
Low season: None
Mailing address: 876 Westview Crescent, North Vancouver,
 B.C., V7N 3Y2 Canada
Telephone: (604) 987–7635

58° 22' North Sailing Charters
Cruising area: Alaska
Types of charters: Bareboat, crewed
Boat length: 30 and 36 feet
Number of boats: 2
High season: June 1–August 31
Low season: May 15–May 31 and September 1–September 15
Mailing address: P.O. Box 32391, Juneau, AK 99803
Telephone: (907) 789–7301

Harbor Sailboats
Cruising area: San Diego
Types of charters: Bareboat, crewed, sailing/cruising school
Boat length: 19 to 46 feet
Number of boats: 38
High season: Not available
Low season: Not available
Mailing address: 2040 Harbor Island Drive, San Diego, CA 92101
Telephone: (800) 854–6625 or (619) 291–9568

Island Cruising Ltd.
Cruising area: Gulf and San Juan islands, Desolation Sound
Types of charters: Bareboat, crewed, flotilla, sailing/cruising school
Boat length: 29 to 39 feet
Number of boats: Not available
High season: June 24–September 8
Low season: April 22–June 23 and September 9–April 21
Mailing address: 6145 Genoa Bay Road, RR 1, Duncan, B.C.,

V9L 1M3 Canada
Telephone: (800) 663–5311 or (604) 748–6575
Fax: (604) 748–6950

Marina Sailing

Cruising area: Point Conception, California, to Mexico border
Types of charters: Bareboat, crewed, flotilla
Boat length: 24 to 43 feet
Number of boats: 80
High season: May 1–October 31
Low season: November 1–April 30
Mailing address: 746 Washington Boulevard, Marina Del Rey,
   CA 90292
Telephone: (800) 262–7245 or (213) 822–6617

Marine Adventure Sailing Tours

Cruising area: Alaska
Types of charters: Bareboat, crewed
Boat length: 50 feet
Number of boats: 1
High season: May 1–September 30
Low season: Not available
Mailing address: 945 Fritz Cove Road, Juneau, AK 99801
Telephone: (907) 789–0919

North Isle Sailing

Cruising area: Puget Sound, San Juan Islands, Desolation
   Sound, Gulf Islands
Types of charters: Crewed
Boat length: 36 feet
Number of boats: 1
High season: Not available
Low season: Not available
Mailing address: 2550 North Swantown Road, Oak Harbor, WA
   98277
Telephone: (206) 675–8360

Northwest Marine Charters

Cruising area: Washington state to Alaska

Types of charters: Bareboat, crewed
Boat length: 27 to 127 feet
Number of boats: 19
High season: July 1–September 15
Low season: June 1–June 30 and September 16–September 30
Mailing address: 2400 Westlake Avenue North, Seattle, WA
   98109
Telephone: (800) 659–3048 or (206) 283–3040

Pacific Quest Charters
Cruising area: San Juan Islands to Vancouver Island
Types of charters: Bareboat, crewed
Boat length: 27 to 44 feet
Number of boats: 27
High season: June 27–September 7
Low season: April 16–June 26 and September 8–October 13
Mailing address: 1521 Foreshore Walk, Granville Island,
   Vancouver, B.C., V6H 3X3 Canada
Telephone: (604) 682–2161 or (604) 682–5312
Fax: (604) 682–2722

Pacific Yachting
Cruising area: Monterey Bay, California
Types of charters: Bareboat, crewed, flotilla, sailing/cruising school
Boat length: 25 to 43 feet
Number of boats: 15
High season: March 1–December 1
Low season: December 1–February 28
Mailing address: 333 Lake Avenue, Santa Cruz, CA 95062
Telephone: (800) 374–2626 or (408) 476–2370

Penmar Marine Company
Cruising area: Puget Sound to Alaska
Types of charters: Bareboat, crewed, flotilla
Boat length: 25 to 65 feet
Number of boats: 80
High season: June 20–September 12
Low season: September 15–June 19
Mailing address: 2011 Skyline Way, Anacortes, WA 98221

Telephone: (800) 828–7337 or (206) 293–4839
Fax: (206) 293–2427

Peter Falk & Associates
Cruising area: Pacific Northwest, Virgin Islands
Types of charters: Crewed
Boat length: Not available
Number of boats: Not available
High season: Not available
Low season: Not available
Mailing address: 3333 Noyo Street, Oakland, CA 94602
Telephone: (510) 482–0993
Fax: (510) 482–0997

Sail North
Cruising area: Great Slave Lake
Types of charters: Bareboat
Boat length: Not available
Number of boats: Not available
High and low season: June–August
Mailing address: Box 2497, Yellowknife, Northwest Territories,
   X1A 2P8 Canada
Telephone: (403) 873–8019

San Diego Yacht Charters
Cruising area: Santa Barbara to Ensenada, Mexico
Types of charters: Bareboat, crewed, flotilla, cruising school
Boat length: 24 to 50 feet
Number of boats: 30
High season: Not available
Low season: Not available
Mailing address: 1880 Harbor Island Drive, San Diego, CA 92101
Telephone: (800) 456–0222 or (619) 297–4555
Fax: (619) 297–5856

Seahorse Sailing, Inc.
Cruising area: Puget & Desolation sounds, Gulf & San Juan
   islands
Types of charters: Bareboat, crewed, flotilla

Boat length: 24 to 56 feet
Number of boats: 20
High season: July 1–August 30
Low season: April 1–June 30 and September 1–November 15
Mailing address: 2075 Tryon Road, Sidney, B.C., V8L 3X9
  Canada
Telephone: (604) 655–4979
Fax: (604) 655–4956

Set Sail Yacht Charters
Cruising area: Santa Barbara to Ensenada, Mexico
Types of charters: Bareboat
Boat length: 29 to 48 feet
Number of boats: 18
High season: April 1–September 30
Low season: October 1–March 31
Mailing address: 2131 Shelter Island Drive, San Diego, CA 92106
Telephone: (800) 553–7245 or (619) 224–3791
Fax: (619) 224–8736

Spinnaker Sailing
Cruising area: San Francisco Bay
Types of charters: Bareboat, crewed
Boat length: 21 to 35 feet
Number of boats: 16
High season: March 1–November 14
Low season: November 15–February 28
Mailing address: #1 Uccelli Boulevard, Redwood City, CA 94603
Telephone: (415) 363–1390

Waltzing Bear Sail Charters
Cruising area: Alaska
Types of charters: Bareboat, crewed
Boat length: 30 and 38 feet
Number of boats: 2
High season: June 1–August 31
Low season: April 15–May 31 and September 1–October 30
Mailing address: 4600 Halibut Point Road, Sitka, AK 99835
Telephone: (907) 747–3608

Dall porpoises in Alaskan waters *(Alaskan Wilderness Safaris)*

Wind 'N Sails

Cruising area: San Juan and Gulf islands
Types of charters: Bareboat, crewed, flotilla, sailing/cruising school
Boat length: 18 to 44 feet
Number of boats: 23
High season: June 28–September 5
Low season: May 31–June 26 and September 6–May 31
Mailing address: P.O. Box 337, Friday Harbor, WA 98250
Telephone: (800) 752–4121 or (206) 378–5343

Wind Works Sailing Center, Inc.

Cruising area: Puget Sound, San Juan Islands
Types of charters: Bareboat, crewed, sailing/cruising school
Boat length: 27 to 45 feet
Number of boats: 10
High season: May 1–September 30
Low season: October 1–April 30
Mailing address: 7001 Seaview Avenue NW, Seattle, WA 98117
Telephone: (206) 784–9386

Great Lakes

Adventure Plus Yacht Charters & Sailing School
Cruising area: Lake Erie
Types of charters: Bareboat, crewed, sailing/cruising school
Boat length: 33 to 38 feet
Number of boats: 13
High season: June 1–August 30
Low season: May 1–May 31 and September 1–October 30
Mailing address: 701 East Water Street, Sandusky, OH 44870
Telephone: (419) 624–5000

Apostle Islands Yacht Charter Association
Cruising area: Apostle Islands, Lake Superior
Types of charters: Bareboat, crewed
Boat length: 27 to 45 feet
Number of boats: 24
High season: June 15–September 1
Low season: May 15–June 15 and September 1–October 15
Mailing address: P.O. Box 188, LaPointe, WI 54850
Telephone: (800) 821–3480 or (715) 747–2983

Bay Breeze Sailing Charters
Cruising area: Lake Michigan
Types of charters: Bareboat, crewed, flotilla, sailing/cruising
  school
Boat length: 25 to 44 feet
Number of boats: 6
High season: June 1–August 30
Low season: September 1–September 30
Mailing address: P.O. Box 752, Sturgeon Bay, WI 54235
Telephone: (414) 388–0234

Bay Breeze Yacht Charters
Cruising area: Lake Michigan (Traverse Bay, North Channel)
Types of charters: Bareboat, crewed
Boat length: 27 to 46 feet

Number of boats: 25
High season: June 20–August 29
Low season: May 16–June 19 and September 1–October 30
Mailing address: 12935 West Bay Shore Drive, Suite 200,
  Traverse City, MI 49684
Telephone: (616) 941–0535

Burr Yacht Charters, Inc.

Cruising area: Great Lakes (Erie, Huron, Michigan)
Types of charters: Bareboat, crewed, flotilla
Boat length: 25 to 40 feet
Number of boats: 3
High season: May 1–October 15
Low season: None
Mailing address: 32575 South River Road, Mount Clemens, MI
  48045
Telephone: (800) 445–6592 or (313) 463–8629
Fax: (313) 463–7842

Canadian Power & Sail Charters, Inc.

Cruising area: North Channel & Georgian Bay, Lake Huron
Types of charters: Bareboat, crewed, flotilla
Boat length: 28 to 40 feet
Number of boats: 20
High season: July 1–August 30
Low season: June 1–June 30 and August 1–August 30
Mailing address: RR 2, Minesing, Ontario, L0L 1Y0 Canada
Telephone: (705) 721–4297

Classic Yachts of Door County

Cruising area: Lake Michigan
Types of charters: Bareboat, crewed, flotilla
Boat length: 24 to 41 feet
Number of boats: 7
High season: July 1–August 30
Low season: June 1–June 30 and September 1–September 30
Mailing address: P.O. Box 519, Sturgeon Bay, WI 54235
Telephone: (414) 743–2478
Fax: (414) 743–7280

Discovery Yacht Charters
Cruising area: North Channel and Georgian Bay (Lake Huron), British Virgin Islands
Types of charters: Bareboat
Boat length: 26 to 50 feet
Number of boats: Not available
High season: Lake Huron, June 15–September 8; BVI, December 15–April 12
Low season: Lake Huron, not available; BVI, April 13–December 14
Mailing address: 15 Water Street East, No. 2, Little Current, Ontario, P0P 1KD Canada
Telephone: (800) 268–8222 or (705) 368–3744
Fax: (705) 368–3027

Door County Sailing
Cruising area: Green Bay, Lake Michigan
Types of charters: Bareboat
Boat length: 27 to 35 feet
Number of boats: 6
High season: July 1–August 30
Low season: May 1–June 30 and September 1–October 30
Mailing address: 10967 North Bayshore Drive, Sister Bay, WI 54234
Telephone: (414) 854–2124

Executive Sailing Charters
Cruising area: Toronto and Georgian Bay
Types of charters: Bareboat, crewed
Boat length: 20 to 38 feet
Number of boats: 40
High season: July 1–August 31
Low season: May 1–June 30 and September 1–September 30
Mailing address: 275 Queen's Quay West, Toronto, Ontario M5V 1A2 Canada
Telephone: (416) 947–0333

Fairwind Sail Charters, Inc.
Cruising area: Lake Michigan, Virgin Islands

Types of charters: Bareboat, crewed
Boat length: 28 to 43 feet
Number of boats: 6
High season: Not available
Low season: Not available
Mailing address: 3107 South Morgan Street, Chicago, IL 60608
Telephone: (312) 890–4656

Great Lakes Tall Ship Adventures
Cruising area: Lake Michigan
Types of charters: Crewed
Boat length: 105 and 114 feet
Number of boats: 2
High season: July 1–August 30
Low season: May 1–June 30 and September 1–September 30
Mailing address: 13390 SW Bay Shore Drive, Traverse City, MI
   49684
Telephone: (616) 941–2000
Fax: (616) 941–0520

Harbor North
Cruising area: Lake Erie, Florida Keys
Types of charters: Bareboat, crewed, sailing/cruising school
Boat length: 22 to 38 feet
Number of boats: 25
High season: Lake Erie, May 15–October 31; Florida,
   November 15–May 15
Low season: None
Mailing address: P.O. Box 504, 400 Huron Street, Huron, OH
   44839
Telephone: (800) 451–7245 or (419) 433–4906

Michigan City Sailboat Charters, Inc.
Cruising area: Lake Michigan
Types of charters: Bareboat, crewed, flotilla
Boat length: 27 to 38 feet
Number of boats: 12
High season: June 1–September 30
Low season: May 1–May 31 and October 1–October 31

Mailing address: P.O. Box 8768, Michigan City, IN 46360
Telephone: (219) 879–7608

Northwind Sailing

Cruising area: Lake Superior
Types of charters: Bareboat
Boat length: 23 to 43 feet
Number of boats: 5
High season: June 1–September 15
Low season: None
Mailing address: P.O. Box 973, Grand Marais Harbor, Grand
 Marais, MN 55604
Telephone: (218) 387–1265

Superior Charters, Inc.

Cruising area: Apostle Islands, Lake Superior
Types of charters: Bareboat, crewed
Boat length: 27 to 45 feet
Number of boats: 60
High season: June 24–September 9
Low season: May 21–June 23 and September 10–October 7
Mailing address: Route 1, Box 719, Bayfield, WI 54814
Telephone: (800) 772–5124

U-Sail-It, Inc.

Cruising area: Lake Champlain (U.S. side)
Types of charters: Bareboat
Boat length: 28 to 36 feet
Number of boats: 7
High season: June 16–September 7
Low season: Not available
Mailing address: P.O. Box 54, Colchester, VT 05446
Telephone: (802) 878–8888

Venture Yacht Charters

Cruising area: Lake Ontario, Thousand Islands, Bay of Quinte
Types of charters: Bareboat, sailing school
Boat length: 26 to 39 feet
Number of boats: 8

High season: June 1–September 30
Low season: Not available
Mailing address: Portsmouth Olympic Harbour, 53 Yonge
   Street, Kingston, Ontario, K7M 1E4 Canada
Telephone: (613) 549–1007

White Bay Charters, Inc.
Cruising area: Lake Michigan
Types of charters: Bareboat, crewed
Boat length: 25 to 50 feet
Number of boats: 8
High season: June 1–September 15
Low season: None
Mailing address: 216 South Lake Street, Whitehall, MI 49461
Telephone: (616) 894–4082

Yachting Operations Services
Cruising area: Lake Ontario
Types of charters: Bareboat, crewed, flotilla, sailing school
Boat length: 30 to 42 feet
Number of boats: 5
High season: June 1–August 30
Low season: May 1–May 31 and September 1–September 30
Mailing address: Box 172, Harbor Road, Henderson Harbor, NY
   13651
Telephone: (315) 938–5494
Fax: (315) 938–5536

United States East Coast and Gulf Coast

A-B-Sea Sailing
Cruising area: West coast of Florida and Florida Keys
Types of charters: Bareboat, crewed, flotilla, sailing/cruising school
Boat length: 25 to 44 feet
Number of boats: 30
High season: December 15–May 1
Low season: May 1–December 15
Mailing address: 4995 U.S.Highway 19, New Port Richey, FL 34652
Telephone: (800) 227–5127 or (813) 845–1726

AYS Charters & Sailing School
Cruising area: Chesapeake Bay
Types of charters: Bareboat, sailing/cruising school
Boat length: 28 to 43 feet
Number of boats: 24
High season: May 1–October 15
Low season: April, August, and October 16–October 31
Mailing address: 7416 Edgewood Road, Annapolis, MD 21403
Telephone: (410) 267–8181
Fax: (410) 267–7409

Amarok Sailing Charters
Cruising area: Florida Keys and Bahamas
Types of charters: Crewed
Boat length: 41 feet
Number of boats: 1
High season and low season: Year-round
Mailing address: P.O. Box 45-1305, Miami, FL 33245
Telephone: (305) 934–5547

American Bahamas Charters
Cruising area: Miami, Florida Keys, Bahamas, Virgin Islands

Types of charters: Bareboat, crewed
Boat length: 40 to 83 feet
Number of boats: 20-plus
High season: November 1–May 1
Low season: May 2–October 31
Mailing address: P.O. Box 331072, Coconut Grove, FL 33133
Telephone: (305) 443–8310

Annapolis Bay Charters, Inc.

Cruising area: Chesapeake Bay
Types of charters: Bareboat, crewed, flotilla
Boat length: 27 to 52 feet
Number of boats: 40
High season: April 1–November 30
Low season: None
Mailing address: P.O. Box 4604, Annapolis, MD 21403
Telephone: (410) 269–1776
Fax: (410) 280–5644

Blue Water Yacht Charters

Cruising area: Florida East Coast and Keys, Bahamas
Types of charters: Bareboat, crewed
Boat length: 31 to 49 feet
Number of boats: 12
High season: November 1–May 1
Low season: May 2–October 31
Mailing address: 1414 South Andrews Avenue, Fort Lauderdale,
  FL 33316
Telephone: (800) 522–2992 or (305) 768–0846

Caribbean Soul Charters

Cruising area: Florida Keys
Types of charters: Bareboat
Boat length: 22 feet
Number of boats: 2
High season: November 1–April 30
Low season: May 1–October 31
Mailing address: P.O. Box 2484, Marathon Shores, FL 33052
Telephone: (305) 743–8454

Carolina Wind Yachting Center, Inc.

Cruising area: North Carolina
Types of charters: Bareboat, crewed, flotilla
Boat length: 27 to 39 feet
Number of boats: 7
High season: April 1–November 30
Low season: December 1–March 31
Mailing address: P.O. Box 967, Washington, NC 27889
Telephone: (800) 334–7671 or (919) 946–4653

C&C Charters Ltd.

Cruising area: United States East Coast, Maine to Florida
Types of charters: Bareboat, crewed, flotilla
Boat length: 26 to 46 feet
Number of boats: Not available
High season: May 1–October 30
Low season: Not available
Mailing address: P.O. Box 691, Point Pleasant, NJ 08742
Telephone: (909) 295–3450

C&C Charters Maryland

Cruising area: Chesapeake Bay
Types of charters: Bareboat, crewed
Boat length: 30 to 43 feet
Number of boats: 12
High season: Not available
Low season: Not available
Mailing address: Mears Point Marina, Box 535 AA, Grasonville,
  MD 21638
Telephone: (800) 733–7245 or (410) 827–7888
Fax: (410) 827–5341

Chesapeake Sailing Association

Cruising area: Chesapeake Bay
Types of charters: Bareboat, crewed, sailing school
Boat length: 22 to 43 feet
Number of boats: 10
High season: April 1–November 1
Low season: November 2–March 31

Mailing address: 1525 Bayville Street, Norfolk, VA 23503
Telephone: (800) 768–2022 or (804) 588–2022

Chesapeake Sailing School
Cruising area: Chesapeake Bay
Types of charters: Bareboat, crewed, flotilla, sailing/cruising school
Boat length: 22 to 43 feet
Number of boats: 21
High season: April 1–October 31
Low season: November 1–March 31
Mailing address: 7074 Bembe Beach Road, Annapolis, MD
   21403
Telephone: (800) 776–0012 or (410) 269–1594

Classic Charters
Cruising area: Maine
Types of charters: Bareboat
Boat length: 30 to 47 feet
Number of boats: 20
High season/Low season: June 1–October 1
Mailing address: RR 4, Box 395, Wiscasset, ME 04578
Telephone: (207) 882–5448
Fax: (207) 882–7304

Coastline Sailing School & Yacht Charters
Cruising area: Long Island Sound north to Martha's Vineyard
   and Block Island
Types of charters: Bareboat, crewed, flotilla, sailing/cruising
   school
Boat length: 30 to 45 feet
Number of boats: 13
High season: Not available
Low season: Not available
Mailing address: Eldridge Yard, Marsh Road, Noank, CT 06340
Telephone: (203) 536–2680

Corpus Christi International School of Sailing, Inc.
Cruising area: Texas Gulf coast
Types of charters: Bareboat, crewed, sailing/cruising school

Boat length: 26 to 41 feet
Number of boats: 7
High season: March 1–November 30
Low season: December 1–February 28
Mailing address: Cooper's Alley L-Head, P.O. Box 995, Corpus
    Christi, TX 78403
Telephone: (512) 881–8503

Croton Sailing School, Inc.
Cruising area: Hudson River
Types of charters: Bareboat, crewed, sailing/cruising school
Boat length: 26 to 35 feet
Number of boats: 3
High season: May 1–September 1
Low season: April 1–May 1 and September 1–November 1
Mailing address: P.O. Box 620, Croton-On-Hudson, NY 10520
Telephone: (914) 271–6868

Cruzan Yacht Charters, Inc.
Cruising area: Florida Keys, Bahamas
Types of charters: Bareboat, crewed, flotilla
Boat length: 30 to 50 feet
Number of boats: 6
High season: December 15–May 15
Low season: May 15–December 15
Mailing address: 2270 SW 27 Way, Coconut Grove, FL
    33133
Telephone: (800) 628–0785 or (305) 858–2822

Dodson Boat Sales
Cruising area: New England waters
Types of charters: Bareboat, crewed
Boat length: 34 to 47 feet
Number of boats: 15
High season: July 1–August 31
Low season: May 1–June 15 and October 1–October 31
Mailing address: P.O. Box 272, Stonington, CT 06378
Telephone: (203) 535–1507
Fax: (203) 535–2163

East Passage Sailing, Inc.

Cruising area: Newport, Rhode Island, and 100 miles north or
   south
Types of charters: Bareboat, crewed, sailing school
Boat length: 27 to 42 feet
Number of boats: 12
High season: June 1–Labor Day
Low season: May 1–May 31 and Labor Day–October 15
Mailing address: 1 Lagoon Road, Portsmouth, Rhode Island
   02871
Telephone: (401) 683–5930

Eastern Shore Yacht Charters, Inc.

Cruising area: Chesapeake Bay
Types of charters: Bareboat, crewed, flotilla
Boat length: 28 to 50 feet
Number of boats: 17
High season: April 14–July 7 and August 16–October 15
Low season: July 8–August 15
Mailing address: P.O. Box 589, Oxford, MD 21654
Telephone: (410) 226–5000
Fax: (410) 226–5643

Florida Yacht Charter & Sales, Inc.

Cruising area: Florida Keys, Bahamas
Types of charters: Bareboat, crewed, sailing/cruising school
Boat length: 28 to 52 feet
Number of boats: 20
High season: January 10–April 30
Low season: July 16–September 30
Mailing address: 1290 Fifth Street, Miami Beach, FL 33139
Telephone: (800) 537–0050 or (305) 532–8600
Fax: (305) 672–2039

Florida Yachting Association

Cruising area: West coast of Florida and Florida Keys
Types of charters: Bareboat, crewed, sailing school
Boat length: 20 to 42 feet
Number of boats: 6

High season: December 15–April 30
Low season: May 1–December 14
Mailing address: P.O. Box 6220, Fort Myers, FL 33932
Telephone: (800) 533–8908 or (813) 463–7771

Fort Myers Yacht Charters

Cruising area: West coast of Florida
Types of charters: Bareboat, crewed
Boat length: 27 to 43 feet
Number of boats: 14
High season: December 15–May 31
Low season: June 1–December 14
Mailing address: 14341 Port Comfort Road, Fort Myers, FL 33908
Telephone: (813) 466–1800

Free State Yachts

Cruising area: Chesapeake Bay
Types of charters: Bareboat, crewed
Boat length: 38 to 45 feet
Number of boats: 10
High season: May 1–October 15
Low season: Not available
Mailing address: 64 Old South River Road, Edgewater, MD 21037
Telephone: (410) 266–9060
Fax: (301) 266–8309

Gratitude Boat Sales, Inc.

Cruising area: Chesapeake Bay
Types of charters: Bareboat, crewed
Boat length: 27 to 44 feet
Number of boats: 18
High season: April 15–October 31
Low season: Not available
Mailing address: Lawton Avenue, Rock Hall, MD 21661
Telephone: (310) 639–7111 or (301) 639–7112
Fax: (301) 639–7345

Great River Yacht Charters

Cruising area: Chesapeake Bay

Types of charters: Bareboat, crewed
Boat length: 30 to 40 feet
Number of boats: 7
High season: April 1–July 5 and August 22–October 31
Low season: July 6–August 21
Mailing address: 5649 Walnut Street, Rock Hall, MD 21661
Telephone: (800) 677–2166 or (410) 639–2166

Harbor North

Cruising area: Lake Erie, Florida Keys
Types of charters: Bareboat, crewed, sailing/cruising school
Boat length: 22 to 38 feet
Number of boats: 25
High season: Lake Erie, May 15–October 31; Florida Keys,
   November 15–May 15
Low season: None
Mailing address: P.O. Box 504, 400 Huron Street, OH 44839
Telephone: (800) 451–7245 or (419) 433–4906

Hartge Chesapeake Charters

Cruising area: Chesapeake Bay
Types of charters: Bareboat
Boat length: 28 to 40 feet
Number of boats: 25
High season: April 1–July 31 and September 1–November 15
Low season: August 1–August 30
Mailing address: 4880 Church Lane, Galesville, MD 20765
Telephone: (410) 867–7240
Fax: (410) 867–7139

Haven Charters

Cruising area: Chesapeake Bay
Types of charters: Bareboat
Boat length: 29 to 38 feet
Number of boats: 10
High season: May 9–October 12
Low season: April 1–May 9 and October 13–November 30
Mailing address: 20846 Rock Hall Avenue, Rock Hall, MD 21661
Telephone: (410) 639–7140

Havre de Grace Sailing Services, Inc.
Cruising area: Chesapeake Bay
Types of charters: Bareboat, crewed, flotilla, sailing/cruising school
Boat length: 28 to 42 feet
Number of boats: 12
High season: Not available
Low season: Not available
Mailing address: P.O. Box 441, Havre de Grace, MD 21078-0441
Telephone: (800) 526–1528 or (410) 939–2869

Highspire Yacht Charters
Cruising area: Chesapeake Bay
Types of charters: Bareboat, crewed, flotilla
Boat length: 28 to 44 feet
Number of boats: 32
High and low season: Not available
Mailing address: P.O. Box 4249, Annapolis, MD 21403
Telephone: (410) 263–2838

Hinckley Yacht Charters
Cruising area: Maine
Types of charters: Bareboat
Boat length: 30 to 44 feet
Number of boats: 30
High season: July 13–September 12
Low season: Not available
Mailing address: Bass Harbor, ME 04653
Telephone: (207) 244–5008
Fax: (207) 244–7535

Holladay Marine
Cruising area: Maine
Types of charters: Bareboat, crewed
Boat length: 30 and 34 feet
Number of boats: 2
High season: June 1–October 1
Low season: None

Schooner and Caribbean sunset *(Easy Sailing Yacht Charters)*

Mailing address: West Boothbay Harbor, ME 04575
Telephone: (207) 633–4767

J & S Charters

Cruising area: Chesapeake Bay, Florida Keys
Types of charters: Bareboat
Boat length: 31 feet
Number of boats: 2
High season: Chesapeake Bay, May 1–September 30; Florida
  Keys, October 1–May 31
Low season: Not available
Mailing address: 4806 York Road, Baltimore, MD 21212
Telephone: (410) 323–5956
Fax: (410) 377–3080

Jamestown Sailing Charters

Cruising area: New England
Types of charters: Bareboat
Boat length: 36 feet
Number of boats: 1
High season: June 1–September 30
Low season: None
Mailing address: 135 Longfellow Road, Jamestown, RI 02835
Telephone: (401) 423–2619

Kathleen Young Yacht Charters
Cruising area: Florida, Bahamas, Virgin Islands
Types of charters: Bareboat, crewed, flotilla, sailing/cruising school
Boat length: 32 to 54 feet
Number of boats: 27
High season: November 1–April 30
Low season: May 1–October 31
Mailing address: 1326 SE Seventeenth Street, Suite 513, Fort Lauderdale, FL 33316
Telephone: (800) 447–2458 or (305) 768–9737
Fax: (305) 764–6416

La Gringa Sailing Services, Inc.
Cruising area: West coast of Florida, Florida Keys, Dry Tortugas
Types of charters: Bareboat
Boat length: 20 to 41 feet
Number of boats: 5
High season: November 1–May 31
Low season: June 1–October 31
Mailing address: 400 Second Avenue NE, #11, St. Petersburg, FL 33701
Telephone: (813) 822–4323

Landfall Charter Services
Cruising area: Bahamas, Florida Keys
Types of charters: Bareboat
Boat length: 39 to 50 feet
Number of boats: 6
High season: November 15–April 15
Low season: April 16–November 14
Mailing address: P.O. Box 030402, Fort Lauderdale, FL 33303
Telephone: (800) 255–1840 or (305) 763–8464

Moonraker Sailing Charters
Cruising area: Florida Keys, Bahamas
Types of charters: Crewed
Boat length: 48 feet
Number of boats: 1

High season: Year-round
Low season: None
Mailing address: P.O. Box 2924, Key Largo, FL 33037
Telephone: (305) 451–2135

Morris Yacht Charters

Cruising area: Maine
Types of charters: Bareboat
Boat length: 26 to 36 feet
Number of boats: 7
High season: July 15–September 12
Low season: May 1–July 15 and September 12–October 15
Mailing address: P.O. Box 58, Clark Point Road, Southwest
   Harbor, ME 04679
Telephone: (207) 244–5509
Fax: (207) 244–5866

O'Leary's Sailing School & Charters

Cruising area: Florida Keys, Bahamas
Types of charters: Crewed, sailing school
Boat length: 42 feet
Number of boats: 2
High season: Not available
Low season: Not available
Mailing address: 7601 East Treasure Drive, Flamingo Marina, FL
   33141
Telephone: (305) 865–7245

Oyster Bay Sailing School

Cruising area: United States East Coast
Types of charters: Bareboat, crewed, flotilla, sailing school
Boat length: 27 to 40 feet
Number of boats: 30
High season: May 15–September 30
Low season: April 1–May 14 and October 1–October 31
Mailing address: West End Avenue, P.O. Box 447, Oyster Bay,
   NY 11771
Telephone: (800) 323–2207 or (516) 624–7900
Fax: (516) 922–4502

Oz Yacht Charters

Cruising area: East coast of Florida, Florida Keys, Bahamas
Types of charters: Bareboat, crewed, flotilla
Boat length: 38 to 60 feet
Number of boats: 25
High season: November 15–March 31
Low season: April 1–November 14
Mailing address: 1323 SE Seventeenth Street, Suite #437, Fort Lauderdale, FL 33316
Telephone: (800) 999–7245 or (305) 463–0220
Fax: (305) 463–7311

Pelorus Marina, Inc.

Cruising area: Chesapeake Bay
Types of charters: Bareboat, crewed
Boat length: 32 to 42 feet
Number of boats: 7
High season: May 1–June 30 and September 1–October 31
Low season: July 1–August 30
Mailing address: RD #1, Bayside Avenue, Rock Hall, MD 21661
Telephone: (410) 639–2151

Pleiades Yacht Charters

Cruising area: Chesapeake Bay
Types of charters: Bareboat, crewed
Boat length: 32 to 40 feet
Number of boats: 8
High season: April 1–November 30
Low season: None
Mailing address: 9413 Bulls Run Parkway, Bethesda, MD 20817
Telephone: (301) 530–8075

Sail Westbrook, Inc.

Cruising area: Long Island Sound to Newport, Rhode Island; Nantucket; Cape Cod
Types of charters: Bareboat, crewed
Boat length: 31 to 42 feet
Number of boats: Not available

High season: Not available
Low season: Not available
Mailing address: P.O. Box 1179, Westbrook, CT 06498
Telephone: (203) 399–5515
Fax: (203) 399–8076

The Sailing Place, Inc.
Cruising area: North Carolina, Chesapeake Bay, Florida
Types of charters: Bareboat, crewed, flotilla, sailing school
Boat length: 26 to 34 feet
Number of boats: 9
High season: May 1–September 30
Low season: October 1–April 30
Mailing address: 136 Atlantic Beach Causeway, Atlantic Beach, NC 28512
Telephone: (919) 726–5664

Sailing Ventures
Cruising area: Florida Keys, Bahamas, Virgin Islands
Types of charters: Bareboat
Boat length: 19 to 52 feet
Number of boats: 30
High season: December 15–April 15
Low season: April 16–December 14
Mailing address: P.O. Box 921022, Norcross, GA 30092
Telephone: (404) 594–7232

St. Petersburg Yacht Charters
Cruising area: Florida Keys, Dry Tortugas
Types of charters: Bareboat, crewed
Boat length: 28 to 57 feet
Number of boats: 12
High season: December 15–May 15
Low season: May 16–December 14
Mailing address: 55 First Avenue SE, St. Petersburg, FL 33701
Telephone: (813) 823–2555

Seguin Navigation Sailing Charters
Cruising area: Maine

Types of charters: Crewed
Boat length: 16 to 30 feet
Number of boats: 3
High season: Not available
Low season: Not available
Mailing address: HC 33, Box 24-A, Arrowsic, ME 04530
Telephone: (207) 443–1677

Southernmost Sailing, Inc.

Cruising area: Florida Keys
Types of charters: Bareboat
Boat length: 26 to 42 feet
Number of boats: 15
High season: November 1–April 30
Low season: May 1–October 31
Mailing address: P.O. Box 369, Key West, FL 33041
Telephone: (305) 745–2430

Southern Yacht Charters, Inc.

Cruising area: Panama City, Florida, to New Orleans, Louisiana
Types of charters: Bareboat, crewed
Boat length: 30 to 44 feet
Number of boats: 13
High season: March 1–December 1
Low season: December 2–February 28
Mailing address: P.O. Box 1492, Fairhope, AL 36533
Telephone: (800) 458–7245 or (205) 928–1283

Southwest Florida Yachts, Inc.

Cruising area: West coast of Florida
Types of charters: Bareboat, crewed
Boat length: 27 to 44 feet
Number of boats: 20
High season: December 15–April 30
Low season: May 1–December 14
Mailing address: 3444 Marinatown Lane, Suite 19, North Fort
   Myers, FL 33903
Telephone: (800) 262–7939 or (813) 656–1339
Fax: (813) 656–2628

Spindrift Cruises, Inc.
Cruising area: Maine
Types of charters: Bareboat, crewed
Boat length: 24 to 37 feet
Number of boats: 8
High season: June 13–September 26
Low season: May 16–June 12 and September 27–October 10
Mailing address: HCR 35, Box 399, Tenants Harbor, ME 04860
Telephone: (207) 372–6245

Texas Sailing Academy
Cruising area: Lake Travis, Texas
Types of charters: Bareboat, crewed, flotilla, sailing school
Boat length: 19 to 42 feet
Number of boats: 9
High season: April 1–September 30
Low season: October 1–March 31
Mailing address: P.O. Box 5700, Austin, TX 78734
Telephone: (512) 261–6193

Treasure Harbor Marine, Inc.
Cruising area: Florida Keys, Bahamas
Types of charters: Bareboat, crewed
Boat length: 19 to 41 feet
Number of boats: 15
High season: November 15–April 29
Low season: May 1–November 14
Mailing address: 200 Treasure Harbor Drive, Islamorada, FL 33036
Telephone: (800) 352–2628 or (305) 852–2458

Wanderlust Charters, Inc.
Cruising area: Florida, Florida Keys, Bahamas
Types of charters: Bareboat, crewed
Boat length: 30 to 41 feet
Number of boats: 3
High season: Year-round
Low season: None

Mailing address: 4401 NE Thirtieth Avenue, Lighthouse Point, FL 33064
Telephone: (305) 941–1379

Whittaker Creek Yacht Sales & Charters
Cruising area: North Carolina
Types of charters: Bareboat, crewed, flotilla
Boat length: 23 to 46 feet
Number of boats: 13
High season: March 15–November 15
Low season: November 16–March 14
Mailing address: P.O. Box 357, Oriental, NC 28571
Telephone: (800) 525–7245 or (919) 249–0666

Yacht Services International
Cruising area: Maine to North Carolina
Types of charters: Bareboat, crewed, flotilla, sailing/cruising school
Boat length: 29 to 46 feet
Number of boats: 6
High season: Not available
Low season: Not available
Mailing address: P.O. Box 703 Green Brook, NJ 08812
Telephone. (908) 752–1463 or (212) 885–3294

Yachting Vacations, Inc.
Cruising area: West coast of Florida
Types of charters: Bareboat, flotilla
Boat length: 30 to 41 feet
Number of boats: 15
High season: December 1–May 31
Low season: June 1–November 30
Mailing address: 3162 Matecumbe Key Road, Punta Gorda, FL 33955
Telephone: (800) 447–0080

The Caribbean

Abaco Bahamas Charters, Ltd.
Cruising area: Abacos, Bahamas
Types of charters: Bareboat
Boat length: 33 and 44 feet
Number of boats: 14
High season: December 15–July 15
Low season: July 16–December 14
Mailing address: 10905 Cowgill Place, Louisville, KY 40243–1711
Telephone: (800) 626–5690 or (502) 245– 9428
Fax: (502) 245–1537

Amarok Sailing Charters
Cruising area: Florida Keys and Bahamas
Types of charters: Crewed
Boat length: 41 feet
Number of boats: 1
High season/Low season: Year-round
Mailing address: P.O. Box 45-1305, Miami, FL 33245
Telephone: (305) 934–5547

American Bahamas Charters
Cruising area: Miami, Florida Keys, Bahamas, Virgin Islands
Types of charters: Bareboat, crewed
Boat length: 40 to 83 feet
Number of boats: 20-plus
High season: November 1–May 1
Low season: May 2–October 31
Mailing address: P.O. Box 331072, Coconut Grove, FL 33133
Telephone: (305) 443–8310

ATM Yachts
Cruising area: Caribbean (St. Martin, Guadeloupe, Martinique, Leeward Islands, Pacific (French Polynesia), Mediterranean (Marseille)

Types of charters: Bareboat, crewed (flotilla in Martinique only)
Boat length: 36 to 55 feet
Number of boats: Varies by location from 12 to 200
High season: Caribbean, December 20–May 3; French
   Polynesia, July 1–August 31; Mediterranean, not available
Low season: Caribbean, May 4–December 19; French Polynesia,
   September 1–June 30; Mediterranean, not available
Mailing address: 2280 University Drive, Suite 102, Newport
   Beach, CA 92660
Telephone: (800) 634–8822 or (714) 650–0889
Fax: (714) 642–1318

Barefoot Yacht Charters

Cruising area: Martinique to Grenada
Types of charters: Bareboat, crewed, flotilla
Boat length: 33 to 50 feet
Number of boats: 19
High season: December 15–April 4
Low season: April 5–October 31
Mailing address: 21961 U.S. 19 North, Clearwater, FL 34625
Telephone: (800) 677–3195
Fax: (813) 797–3195

Bitter End Yacht Club

Cruising area: British Virgin Islands
Types of charters: Bareboat
Boat length: 24 to 30 feet
Number of boats: 8
High season: December 22–April 7
Low season: April 8–December 21
Mailing address: 875 North Michigan Avenue, Chicago, IL 60611
Telephone: (800) 872–2392 or (312) 944–5855
Fax: (312) 944–2860

Blue Water Yacht Charters

Cruising area: Florida east coast and Keys, Bahamas
Types of charters: Bareboat, crewed
Boat length: 31 to 49 feet
Number of boats: 12

High season: November 1–May 1
Low season: May 2–October 31
Mailing address: 1414 South Andrews Avenue, Fort Lauderdale, FL 33316
Telephone: (800) 522–2992 or (305) 768–0846

Caribbean Adventures
Cruising area: British and U.S. Virgin Islands (for crewed charters, entire Caribbean)
Types of charters: Bareboat, crewed, flotilla
Boat length: 35 to 72 feet
Number of boats: 14
High season: December 15–April 14
Low season: April 15–December 14
Mailing address: P.O. Box 9997, Yacht Haven Marina, St. Thomas, USVI 00801
Telephone: (800) 626–4517 or (809) 776–7245

Caribbean Sailing Charters
Cruising area: British and U.S. Virgin Islands
Types of charters: Bareboat, crewed
Boat length: 33 to 50 feet
Number of boats: 18
High season: December 15–April 15
Low season: April 16–July 31 and November 1–December 14
Mailing address: 3883 Andrews Crossing, Roswell, GA 30075
Telephone: (800) 824–1331 or (404) 641–9640
Fax: (404) 992–0276

Caribbean Yacht Charters, Inc.
Cruising area: British Virgin Islands
Types of charters: Bareboat, crewed, flotilla
Boat length: 38 to 52 feet
Number of boats: 42
High season: December 18–March 30
Low season: May 1–December 17
Mailing address: P.O. Box 583, Marblehead, MA 01945
Telephone: (800) 225–2520 or (617) 599–7990
Fax: (617) 639–0216

Conch Charters Ltd.

Cruising area: British Virgin Islands
Types of charters: Bareboat
Boat length: 30 to 51 feet
Number of boats: Not available
High season: December 16–April 7
Low season: April 8–December 15
Mailing address: 19 Donegani Avenue, Suite 207, Pointe Claire,
  Quebec, H9R 2VC Canada
Telephone: (514) 630–4802

Cruzan Yacht Charters, Inc.

Cruising area: Florida Keys, Bahamas
Types of charters: Bareboat, crewed, flotilla
Boat length: 30 to 50 feet
Number of boats: 6
High season: December 15–May 15
Low season: May 16–December 14
Mailing address: 2270 SW 27 Way, Coconut Grove, FL 33133
Telephone: (800) 628–0785 or (305) 858–2822

Discovery Yacht Charters

Cruising area: North Channel and Georgian Bay (Lake Huron),
  British Virgin Islands
Types of charters: Bareboat
Boat length: 26 to 50 feet
Number of boats: Not available
High season: Lake Huron, June 15–September 8; BVI,
  December 15–April 12
Low season: Lake Huron, not available; BVI, April 13–December
  14
Mailing address: 15 Water Street, East #2, Little Current,
  Ontario, P0P 1KD Canada
Telephone: (800) 268–8222 or (705) 368–3744
Fax: (705) 368–3027

Easy Sailing Yacht Charters

Cruising area: Bahamas
Types of charters: Bareboat, crewed, flotilla

Boat length: 30 to 46 feet
Number of boats: 33
High season: October 1–April 30
Low season: May 1–September 30
Mailing address: P.O. Box 95, Coconut Grove, FL 33133
Telephone: (800) 780–4001

Enterprise Sailing
Cruising area: Balearic Islands, Italy, Sardinia, Greece, Turkey,
  British Virgin Islands
Types of charters: Bareboat, crewed
Boat length: 28 to 45 feet
Number of boats: 80
High season: July 1–September 1
Low season: September 2–June 30
Mailing address: 36 Hart Street, Henvey-On-Thames, Oxon.
  RG9 2AU, England
Telephone: 44–491–410411

Fairwind Sail Charters, Inc.
Cruising area: Lake Michigan, Virgin Islands
Types of charters: Bareboat, crewed
Boat length: 28 to 43 feet
Number of boats: 6
High season: Not available
Low season: Not available
Mailing address: 3107 South Morgan Street, Chicago, IL 60608
Telephone: (312) 890–4656

Florida Yacht Charter & Sales, Inc.
Cruising area: Florida Keys, Bahamas
Types of charters: Bareboat, crewed, sailing/cruising school
Boat length: 28 to 52 feet
Number of boats: 20
High season: January 10–April 30
Low season: July 16–September 30
Mailing address: 1290 Fifth Street, Miami, FL 33139
Telephone: (800) 537–0050 or (305) 532–8600
Fax: (305) 672–2039

Island Yachts

Cruising area: British and U.S. Virgin Islands
Types of charters: Bareboat, crewed, flotilla
Boat length: 30 to 50 feet
Number of boats: 14
High season: December 15–April 14
Low season: August 1–October 31
Mailing address: 6807 Estate Smith Bay, 18-B Red Hook
    Quarter, Charlotte Amalie, St. Thomas, USVI 00802-3201
Telephone: (800) 524–2019

Jet Sea

Cruising area: Bahamas, Guadeloupe, St. Martin
Types of charters: Bareboat, crewed, flotilla
Boat length: 35 to 59 feet
Number of boats: 191
High season: January 1–April 30
Low season: May 1–December 31
Mailing address: 1650 SE Seventeenth Street, Fort Lauderdale,
    FL 33316
Telephone: (800) 262–5382 or (305) 467–0528
Fax: (305) 467–6661

Kathleen Young Yacht Charters

Cruising area: Florida, Bahamas, Virgin Islands
Types of charters: Bareboat, crewed, flotilla, sailing/cruising school
Boat length: 32 to 54 feet
Number of boats: 27
High season: November 1–April 30
Low season: May 1–October 31
Mailing address: 1326 SE Seventeenth Street, Suite 513, Fort
    Lauderdale, FL 33316
Telephone: (800) 447–2458 or (305) 768–9737
Fax: (305) 764–6416

Landfall Charter Services

Cruising area: Bahamas, Florida Keys
Types of charters: Bareboat
Boat length: 39 to 50 feet

Number of boats: 6
High season: November 15–April 15
Low season: April 16–November 14
Mailing address: P.O. Box 030402, Fort Lauderdale, FL 33303
Telephone: (800) 255–1840 or (305) 763–8464

Latitude 18°

Cruising area: British and U.S. Virgin Islands
Types of charters: Bareboat, crewed
Boat length: 28 to 47 feet
Number of boats: 12
High season: December 15–April 14
Low season: April 15–December 14
Mailing address: Box 88, Red Hook, St. Thomas, USVI 00802
Telephone: (809) 775–9964

Leeward Islands Charters

Cruising area: Leeward Islands
Types of charters: Crewed
Boat length: 47 and 70 feet
Number of boats: 2
High season: November 1–May 31
Low season: June 1–October 31
Mailing address: P.O. Box 586, Basseterre, St. Kitts, USVI
Telephone: (809) 465–7474

Melford Pier Ltd.

Cruising area: Scotland, Bahamas
Types of charters: Crewed
Boat length: 50 feet
Number of boats: 2
High season: Scotland, June 1–September 30; Bahamas, year-round
Low season: Scotland, April 1–May 31 and October 1–October 30
Mailing address: Kilmelford by Oban, Argyll, PA34 4XD, Scotland
Telephone: 44–85–22333
Fax: 44–85–22339

Misty Isle Yacht Charters

Cruising area: British and U.S. Virgin Islands

Types of charters: Bareboat, crewed, flotilla
Boat length: 30 to 46 feet
Number of boats: 20
High season: December 15–April 15
Low season: April 16–December 14
Mailing address: P.O. Box 1118, Virgin Gorda, Yacht Harbour, BVI
Telephone: (809) 495–5643
Fax: (809) 495–5300

Moonraker Sailing Charters

Cruising area: Florida Keys, Bahamas
Types of charters: Crewed
Boat length: 48 feet
Number of boats: 1
High season: Year-round
Low season: None
Mailing address: P.O. Box 2924, Key Largo, FL 33037
Telephone: (305) 451–2135

The Moorings

Cruising area: British Virgin Islands, Bahamas, Martinique to Grenada, St. Martin, Guadeloupe, Sea of Cortez, Tahiti, Tonga, Thailand, Greece, Turkey, Yugoslavia, Corsica, Brittany, Spain, Italy, France
Types of charters: Bareboat, crewed, flotilla
Boat length: Varies by location (27 to 60 feet)
Number of boats: Varies by location (600-plus)
High season: Varies by location
Low season: Varies by location
Mailing address: 19345 U.S. 19 North, Clearwater, FL 34624
Telephone: (800) 535–7289 or (813) 530–5424
Fax: (813) 530–9747

Nautor's Swan Charters

Cruising area: Virgin Islands
Types of charters: Bareboat, crewed, flotilla
Boat length: 36 to 61 feet
Number of boats: 24

High season: November 15–May 15
Low season: May 16–November 14
Mailing address: B.P. 335, Marigot 97150, St. Martin, French
   West Indies
Telephone: 590–87–35–48; in the United States, (800)
   356–7926
Fax: 590–87–35–50; in the United States, (401) 846–7349

North South Vacations
Cruising area: British Virgin Islands
Types of charters: Bareboat, crewed
Boat length: 35 to 51 feet
Number of boats: 45
High season: February 1–March 30
Low season: May 1–October 1
Mailing address: 655 Dixon Road, #18, Toronto, Ontario, M9W
   1J4 Canada
Telephone: (800) 387–4964 or (416) 242–7426
Fax: (416) 242–8122

Oasis Marigot
Cruising area: Martinique, St. Lucia, Grenadine Islands
Types of charters: Crewed
Boat length: 40 feet
Number of boats: 2
High season: December 20–April 10
Low season: April 11–December 19
Mailing address: P.O. Box 356, Ahuntsic, Montreal, H3L
   3N9 Canada
Telephone: (514) 381–4383
Fax: (514) 337–8510

Ocean Incentives
Cruising area: British and U.S. Virgin Islands
Types of charters: Bareboat, crewed, flotilla
Boat length: 39 to 51 feet
Number of boats: 9
High season: December 15–April 15
Low season: July 16–October 14

Mailing address: American Yacht Harbor, Red Hook, St.
  Thomas, USVI 00802
Telephone: (800) 344–5762

Offshore Sail & Motor Yachts
Cruising area: British and U.S. Virgin Islands
Types of charters: Bareboat, crewed, flotilla
Boat length: 36 to 54 feet
Number of boats: 20
High season: November 1–February 28
Low season: March 1–October 31
Mailing address: P.O. Box 281, Road Town, Tortola, BVI
Telephone: (809) 494–4726
Fax: (809) 494–3866

O'Leary's Sailing School & Charters
Cruising area: Florida Keys, Bahamas
Types of charters: Crewed, sailing school
Boat length: 42 feet
Number of boats: 2
High season: Not available
Low season: Not available

British Virgin Islands *(Caribbean Yacht Charters, Inc.)*

Mailing address: 7601 East Treasure Drive, Flamingo Marina, FL 33141
Telephone: (305) 865–7245

Oz Yacht Charters
Cruising area: East coast of Florida, Florida Keys, Bahamas
Types of charters: Bareboat, crewed, flotilla
Boat length: 38 to 60 feet
Number of boats: 25
High season: November 15–March 31
Low season: April 1–November 14
Mailing address: 1323 SE Seventeenth Street, Suite #437, Fort Lauderdale, FL 33316
Telephone: (800) 999–7245 or (305) 463–0220
Fax: (305) 463–7311

Peter Falk & Associates
Cruising area: Pacific Northwest, Virgin Islands
Types of charters: Crewed
Boat length: Not available
Number of boats: Not available
High season/Low season: Not available
Mailing address: 3333 Noyo Street, Oakland, CA 94602
Telephone: (510) 482–0993
Fax: (510) 482–0997

Proper Yachts
Cruising area: British and U.S. Virgin Islands
Types of charters: Bareboat, crewed
Boat length: 40 to 51 feet
Number of boats: 8
High season: November 15–April 30
Low season: May 1–November 14
Mailing address: P.O. Box 70, Cruz Bay, St. John, USVI 00830
Telephone: (809) 776–6256
Fax: (809) 776–7406

Sailing Ventures
Cruising area: Florida Keys, Bahamas, Virgin Islands

Types of charters: Bareboat
Boat length: 19 to 52 feet
Number of boats: 30
High season: December 15–April 15
Low season: April 16–December 14
Mailing address: P.O. Box 921022, Norcross, GA 30092
Telephone: (404) 594–7232

Seabreeze Yacht Charters Ltd.
Cruising area: Virgin Islands, Grenadine Islands
Types of charters: Bareboat, crewed
Boat length: 30 to 45 feet
Number of boats: 42
High season: December 21–May 1
Low season: May 2–December 20
Mailing address: 150 Consumers Road, Suite 307, Willowdale,
    Ontario, M2J 1P9 Canada
Telephone: (416) 499–3102

Sharing Yacht Charters
Cruising area: British and U.S. Virgin Islands
Types of charters: Bareboat
Boat length: 32 to 51 feet
Number of boats: 16
High season: Not available
Low season: Not available
Mailing address: Thomas Cook Travel, 100 Cambridge Park
    Drive, Cambridge, MA 02143
Telephone: (800) 234–9959

Signature Yacht Charters
Cruising area: Puerto Rico, Virgin Islands, St. Martin Grenadine
    Islands
Types of charters: Bareboat
Boat length: 38 to 58 feet
Number of boats: 45
High season: December 2–January 4 and January 25–April 4
Low season: May 16–November 30

Mailing address: 164 Eglinton Avenue East, Suite 200, Toronto,
M4P 1G4 Canada
Telephone: (800) 388–1368

Sunsail
Cruising area: Bahamas, British and U.S. Virgin Islands, St.
Martin, Anguilla, St. Barts, Antigua, Martinique to Grenada,
Corsica, Sardinia, Greece, Turkey, Yugoslavia, Thailand
Types of charters: Bareboat, crewed, flotilla
Boat length: 29 to 56 feet
Number of boats: Varies by location (7 to 50)
High season and low season: Varies by location
Mailing address: 2 Prospect Park, 3347 NW Fifty-fifth Street,
Fort Lauderdale, FL 33309
Telephone: (800) 327–2276

Tortola Marine Management Ltd.
Cruising area: British and U.S. Virgin Islands
Types of charters: Bareboat
Boat length: 33 to 51 feet
Number of boats: 30
High season: December 20–March 31
Low season: July 1–October 31
Mailing address: Norwalk Cove Marina, Beach Road, East
Norwalk, CT 06855
Telephone: (800) 633–0155 or (203) 854–5131
Fax: (203) 838–9756

Trade Wind Yachts, Inc.
Cruising area: St. Lucia, Martinique, Grenadine Islands
Types of charters: Bareboat, crewed, sailing/cruising school
Boat length: 31 to 51 feet
Number of boats: 21
High season: January 6–March 31
Low season: June 1–October 31
Mailing address: P.O. Box 1186, Gloucester, VA 23061
Telephone: (800) 825–7245
Fax: (804) 694–0881

Treasure Harbor Marine, Inc.
Cruising area: Florida, Florida Keys, Bahamas
Types of charters: Bareboat, crewed
Boat length: 19 to 41 feet
Number of boats: 15
High season: November 15–April 29
Low season: May 1–November 14
Mailing address: 200 Treasure Harbor Drive, Islamorada, FL 33036
Telephone: (800) 352–2628 or (305) 8552–2458

Trimarine Boat Co. Ltd.
Cruising area: British Virgin Islands, Galapagos
Types of charters: Crewed
Boat length: 95 and 105 feet
Number of boats: 2
High season: Not available
Low season: Not available
Mailing address: P.O. Box 362, Road Town, Tortola, BVI
Telephone: (809) 494–2490
Fax: (809) 494–5774

Tropic Island Yacht Management Ltd.
Cruising area: British and U.S. Virgin Islands
Types of charters: Bareboat, crewed
Boat length: 30 to 51 feet
Number of boats: 30
High season: December 16–April 1
Low season: July 1–November 6
Mailing address: P.O. Box 532, Maya Cove, Tortola, BVI
Telephone: (809) 494–2450
Fax: (809) 495–2155

Wanderlust Charters, Inc.
Cruising area: Florida, Florida Keys, Bahamas
Types of charters: Bareboat, crewed
Boat length: 30 to 41 feet
Number of boats: 3
High season: Year-round
Low season: None

Mailing address: 4401 NE Thirtieth Avenue, Lighthouse Point, FL 33064
Telephone: (305) 941–1379

Windward Yachts Ltd.
Cruising area: Virgin Islands to Grenada
Types of charters: Bareboat, crewed
Boat length: 42 to 65 feet
Number of boats: 5
High season: Not available
Low season: Not available
Mailing address: 29 Eastern Parade, Fareham, Hants PO16 0RL, England
Telephone: 44–329–236920
Fax: 44–329–823577

Yacht Connections Ltd.
Cruising area: Virgin Islands, Leeward and Windward Islands, France, Italy, Balearic Islands, Yugoslavia, Greece, Turkey, Seychelles, Thailand
Types of charters: Crewed
Boat length: 40 to 75 feet
Number of boats: 100
High season: December 1–May 1
Low season: May 2–November 30
Mailing address: The Hames, 13 Church Road, South Ascot, Berkshire SL5 9DP, England
Telephone: 44–344–24987
Fax: 44–344–26849

Yacht Promenade
Cruising area: British and U.S. Virgin Islands
Types of charters: Crewed
Boat length: 65 feet
Number of boats: 1
High season: December 15–April 30
Low season: May 1–December 14
Mailing address: Box 4065, St. Thomas, USVI 00803
Telephone: (809) 494–3853

Central and South America

Associated Mystic Yacht Charters
Cruising area: Belize
Types of charters: Bareboat, crewed
Boat length: 31 to 55 feet
Number of boats: 4
High season: December 1–April 15
Low season: April 16–November 30
Mailing address: P.O. Box 237, Mystic, CT 06355
Telephone: (800) 873–2692

Cottongim Enterprises
Cruising area: Belize
Types of charters: Crewed
Boat length: 41 feet
Number of boats: 1
High season/Low season: Year-round
Mailing address: Route #2, Salem, IN 47167
Telephone: (812) 883–6602

Golden Pheasant Yacht Charter
Cruising area: Greece, Turkey, Venezuela
Types of charters: Crewed
Boat length: 50 feet
Number of boats: 1
High season: June 1–August 30
Low season: September 1–May 31
Mailing address: 20 Phillimore Gardens, London W8 6S9,
   England
Telephone: 44–71–937–4445

The Moorings
Cruising area: British Virgin Islands, Bahamas, Martinique to
   Grenada, St. Martin, Guadeloupe, Sea of Cortez, Tahiti, Tonga,
   Thailand, Greece, Turkey, Yugoslavia, Corsica, Brittany, Spain,
   Italy, France

Types of charters: Bareboat, crewed, flotilla
Boat length: Varies by location (27 to 60 feet)
Number of boats: Varies by location (600-plus)
High season: Varies by location
Low season: Varies by location
Mailing address: 19345 U.S. 19 North, Clearwater, FL 34624
Telephone: (800) 535–7289 or (813) 530–5424
Fax: (813) 530–9747

San Diego Yacht Charters
Cruising area: Santa Barbara to Ensenada, Mexico
Types of charters: Bareboat, crewed, flotilla, cruising school
Boat length: 24 to 50 feet
Number of boats: 30
High season: Not available
Low season: Not available
Mailing address: 1880 Harbor Island Drive, San Diego, CA
  92101
Telephone: (800) 456–0222 or (619) 297–4555
Fax: (619) 297–5856

Set Sail Yacht Charters
Cruising area: Santa Barbara to Ensenada, Mexico
Types of charters: Bareboat
Boat length: 29 to 48 feet
Number of boats: 18
High season: April 1–September 31
Low season: October 1–March 31
Mailing address: 2131 Shelter Island Drive, San Diego, CA
  92106
Telephone: (800) 553–7245 or (619) 224–3791
Fax: (619) 224–8736

Canary Islands

Club Sail

Cruising area: English Channel, Canary Islands, Madeira
Types of charters: Bareboat, crewed, flotilla, sailing school
Boat length: 33 to 45 feet
Number of boats: 5
High season: UK—May 1–September 30; Canaries—October
  1–March 31
Low season: UK—October 1–April 30; Canaries—May
  1–September 30
Mailing address: The Moorings, 27 Cobbett Road, Southampton
  SO2 4HJ, England
Telephone: 44–703–331856
Fax: 44–703–551167

Gibraltar Sailing Centre

Cruising area: Canary Islands and Madeira
Types of charters: Bareboat, crewed
Boat length: 31 to 45 feet
Number of boats: 12
High season: June 1–September 30
Low season: October 1–December 19
Mailing address: Sheppards Marina, Waterport, Gibraltar
Telephone: 350–78554

Swan Sail Yacht Charter Ltd.

Cruising area: France, Corsica, Balearic Islands, Greece, Turkey,
  Canary Islands, Antilles
Types of charters: Bareboat, crewed
Boat length: 27 to 51 feet
Number of boats: Varies by location
High season and low season: Varies by location
Mailing address: P.O. Box 77, Bury Lancs BL9 7YE, England
Telephone: 44–617–052288
Fax: 44–617–972518

United Kingdom, Ireland, English Channel, and North Sea

ATM Yachts
Cruising area: St. Martin, Guadeloupe, Martinique, Grenadines, Tahiti, France, Spain, Balearic Islands, Corsica, Sardinia
Types of charters: Bareboat, crewed
Boat length: 32 to 72 feet
Number of boats: Varies with area
High season and low season: Varies with area
Low season: Varies with area
Mailing address: Bramling House, Bramling, Canterbury, Kent CT3 1NB, England
Telephone: 44–227–721874 or 44–227–721875
Fax: 44–227–721617

Arcadian Charters
Cruising area: Brest to Elbe
Types of charters: Bareboat, crewed
Boat length: 31 to 41 feet
Number of boats: 14
High season: June 14–September 1
Low season: Not available
Mailing address: 1 Beechcroft, South Town, Dartmouth, Devon TQ6 9BU, England
Telephone: 44–803–834896

Atlantic Adventures
Cruising area: Ireland (west coast)
Types of charters: Bareboat
Boat length: 31 to 39 feet
Number of boats: 5
High season: June 19–August 29
Low season: April 14–June 18 and August 30–October 15
Mailing address: Fances Street, Kilrush, Ireland
Telephone: 353–65–52133
Fax: 353–65–51720

Blakes Holidays

Cruising area: Norfolk Broads (England), Scotland
Types of charters: Bareboat
Boat length: 25 to 32 feet
Number of boats: Not available
High season: June 13–August 22
Low season: April 4–June 16 and August 23–October 31
Mailing address: Wroxham, Norwich NR12 8DH, England
Telephone: 44–603–782141
Fax: 44–603–782871

Blue Peter Yacht Charters

Cruising area: Elbe to Brest and south coast of England
Types of charters: Bareboat, crewed
Boat length: 33 to 47 feet
Number of boats: Not available
High season: May 1–August 30
Low season: April 1–April 30 and September 1–October 30
Mailing address: Deacon's Boatyard, Bursledon, Southampton
  SO3 8AZ, England
Telephone: 44–703–406420

Channel Sailing

Cruising area: North Sea and English Channel
Types of charters: Bareboat, crewed, flotilla
Boat length: 31 to 46 feet
Number of boats: 20
High season and low season: Not available
Mailing address: Sportstraat 272, B-9000, Gent, Belgium
Telephone: 32–91–22–05–71
Fax: 32–91–21–97–38

Club Sail

Cruising area: English Channel, Canary Islands, Madeira
Types of charters: Bareboat, crewed, flotilla, sailing school
Boat length: 33 to 45 feet
Number of boats: 5
High season: UK, May 1–September 30; Canaries, October
  1–March 31

Low season: UK, October 1–April 30; Canaries, May 1–September 30
Mailing address: The Moorings, 27 Cobbett Road, Southampton
  SO2 4HJ, England
Telephone: 44–703–331856
Fax: 44–703–551167

Clyde Offshore Sailing Centre
Cruising area: Scotland
Types of charters: Bareboat, crewed, sailing/cruising school
Boat length: 29 to 42 feet
Number of boats: 12
High season: May 1–September 30
Low season: January 2–March 30 and November 1–December 31
Mailing address: Kip Marina, Inverkip, Renfrewshire PA16 0AS,
  Scotland
Telephone: 44–475–521210
Fax: 44–475–921572

Cornish Cruising
Cruising area: English Channel, Ireland, French coast, Scilly
  Islands, Spain
Types of charters: Bareboat, crewed, sailing/cruising school
Boat length: 21 to 44 feet
Number of boats: 14
High season: July 18 September 11
Low season: April 18–July 17 and September 12–October 2
Mailing address: Old Chapel Yard, Church Street, Falmouth
  TR11 3EF, England
Telephone: 44–326–318309

Crane Yacht Charters
Cruising area: Scotland
Types of charters: Bareboat, crewed
Boat length: 31 to 33 feet
Number of boats: 4
High season: May 1–August 31
Low season: April 1–April 30 and September 1–October 31
Mailing address: 8, Ardayre Road, Prestwick, Ayrshire KA9 1QL
  Scotland

Telephone: 44–292–75355
Fax: 44–292–312836

E.M.E. Yacht Charter
Cruising area: English Channel, Isles of Scilly, Brittany
Types of charters: Bareboat, crewed, flotilla, sailing school
Boat length: 24 to 44 feet
Number of boats: 40
High season: July 11–August 29
Low season: October 10–April 4
Mailing address: Marina House, Falmouth Yacht Marina,
   Falmouth, Cornwall TR11 2TD, England
Telephone and fax: 44–326–211121

Fal Sail
Cruising area: Brest to Elbe
Types of charters: Bareboat, crewed, sailing/cruising school
Boat length: 31 and 32 feet
Number of boats: 2
High season: June 1–September 30
Low season: October 1–May 30
Mailing address: Polkerris, 1 Wood Lane, Falmouth, Cornwall
   TR11 4RG, England
Telephone: 44–326–313208

Fowey Cruising School
Cruising area: English Channel and Brittany
Types of charters: Crewed, sailing school
Boat length: 29 to 36 feet
Number of boats: Not available
High season: April 1–September 30
Low season: March 1–March 31 and October 1–November 30
Mailing address: 32 Fore Street, Fowey, Cornwall PL23 1AQ,
   England
Telephone: 44–726–832129
Fax: 44–726–832000

Hoseasons Holidays Ltd.
Cruising area: Scotland

Types of charters: Bareboat
Boat length: 23 to 36 feet
Number of boats: 10
High season: April 1–October 30
Low season: None
Mailing address: Sunway House, Lowestoft, Suffolk NR32 3LT,
  England
Telephone: 44–502–501010
Fax: 44–502–514298

Impression Marine
Cruising area: Solent, Channel Islands, Brest to Elbe
Types of charters: Bareboat, crewed
Boat length: 28 to 76 feet
Number of boats: 15
High season: June 2–August 30
Low season: October 1–March 31
Mailing address: 2 Exmoor Close, Aikman Lane, Totton,
  Southampton, Hants SO4 2FT, England
Telephone: 44–703–861078

Jersey Yacht Charters
Cruising area: Brittany and Channel Islands
Types of charters: Bareboat, crewed, sailing/cruising school
Boat length: 32 to 44 feet
Number of boats: 6
High season: July 1–August 31
Low season: March 1–June 30 and September 1–October 30
Mailing address: St. Helier Marina, St. Helier, Jersey, Channel
  Islands, Great Britain
Telephone: 44–534–888100
Fax: 44–534–888088

Liberty Yacht Charters
Cruising area: Brittany and Channel Islands
Types of charters: Bareboat, crewed
Boat length: 28 to 44 feet
Number of boats: 15
High season: June 1–August 31

Low season: March 1–May 31 and September 1–October 31
Mailing address: Queen Anne's Battery Marina, Plymouth,
    Devon PL4 0LP, England
Telephone: 44–752–227911
Fax: 44–752–229122

Melfort Pier Ltd.

Cruising area: Scotland, Bahamas
Types of charters: Crewed
Boat length: 50 feet
Number of boats: 2
High season: Scotland, June 1–September 30; Bahamas, year-round
Low season: Scotland, April 1–May 31 and October 1–October 30
Mailing address: Kilmelford by Oban, Argyll PA34 4XD, Scotland
Telephone: 44–8522–333
Fax: 44–8522–329

The Moorings

Cruising area: British Virgin Islands, Bahamas, Martinique to
    Grenada, St. Martin, Guadeloupe, Sea of Cortez, Tahiti, Tonga,
    Thailand, Greece, Turkey, Yugoslavia, Corsica, Brittany, Spain,
    Italy, France
Types of charters: Bareboat, crewed, flotilla
Boat length: 27 to 60 feet
Number of boats: Varies by location (600-plus)
High season and low season: Varies by location
Mailing address: 19345 U.S. 19 North, Clearwater, FL 34624
Telephone: (800) 535–7289 or (813) 530–5424
Fax: (813) 530–9747

Multihull Marketing

Cruising area: English Channel and French coast
Types of charters: Bareboat, crewed
Boat length: 26 to 37 feet
Number of boats: 14
High season: May 1–August 30
Low season: September 1–April 30
Mailing address: Parkstone Poole BHH14 8EE, England
Telephone: 44–202–744501

New Hebridean Cruising Co. Ltd.
Cruising area: Scotland (500-mile radius from Craobh)
Types of charters: Bareboat, crewed
Boat length: 29 to 42 feet
Number of boats: 11
High season: May 1–August 28
Low season: March 20–April 30 and August 29–October 30
Mailing address: Craobh Haven, by Lochgilphead, Argyll PA31
  8UD, Scotland
Telephone: 44–8525–322
Fax: 44–8525–324

1938 Redwings
Cruising area: Poole Harbour, England
Types of charters: Bareboat, crewed, flotilla
Boat length: 28 feet
Number of boats: 13
High season: April 1–October 30
Low season: None
Mailing address: 75 Lake Drive, Hamworthy, Poole, Dorset
  BH15 4LR, England
Telephone: 44–202–672641
Fax: 44–202–668280

Portway Yacht Charters
Cruising area: Elbe to Brest
Types of charters: Bareboat, crewed, flotilla
Boat length: 24 to 58 feet
Number of boats: 40
High season: June 1–August 30
Low season: April 1–May 30 and September 1–October 31
Mailing address: Portway House, 2 Dartside, Totnes, Devon
  TQ9 5HL, England
Telephone: 44–803–866281

Rossbrin Yacht Charters
Cruising area: Ireland
Types of charters: Crewed
Boat length: 36 feet

Number of boats: 1
High season: Not available
Low season: Not available
Mailing address: Rossbrin Cove, Schull, West Cork, Ireland
Telephone: 353–28–37165

Scottish European Charter
Cruising area: Scotland
Types of charters: Bareboat
Boat length: 25 to 39 feet
Number of boats: 12
High season: May 1–August 30
Low season: April 1–April 30 and September 1–October 31
Mailing address: Mid Auchentiber, Auchentiber, Ayrshire KA13 7RR, Scotland
Telephone: 44–294–85278

Sea Jay Charters
Cruising area: English and French coasts
Types of charters: Bareboat, crewed, sailing school
Boat length: 30 to 37 feet
Number of boats: 30
High season: May 1–August 30
Low season: September 1–April 30
Mailing address: 24 Colesbourne Road, Bloxham Banbury, Oxfordshire OX15 4TB, England
Telephone: 44–295–720861

Sea Ventures Ltd.
Cruising area: United Kingdom, Channel Islands, French coast
Types of charters: Bareboat, crewed, sailing school
Boat length: 28 to 46 feet
Number of boats: 17
High season: May 1–August 31
Low season: March 1–April 30 and September 1–October 31
Mailing address: Lymington Yacht Haven, Lymington, Hants SO41 9XY, England
Telephone: 44–590–672472
Fax: 44–590–671924

Seaway Sailing

Cruising area: Solent
Types of charters: Bareboat, crewed
Boat length: 32 to 41 feet
Number of boats: 9
High season: June 1–August 31
Low season: September 1–May 30
Mailing address: Shamrock Quay, William Street, Southampton
SO1 1QL, England
Telephone: 44–703–234666
Fax: 44–703–234270

Skyes'l Charters

Cruising area: Scotland (west coast)
Types of charters: Crewed
Boat length: 50 and 60 feet
Number of boats: 2
High season: June 1–August 30
Low season: April 1–May 31 and September 1–September 30
Mailing address: 36, Bernisdale, Portree, Isle of Skye IV51 9NS,
Scotland
Telephone: 44–47–032413

Sleat Marine Services

Cruising area: Scotland
Types of charters: Bareboat, crewed
Boat length: 34 to 45 feet
Number of boats: 7
High season: May 16–August 22
Low season: March 21–May 9 and August 23–September 26
Mailing address: Ardvasar, Isle of Skye IV45 8RU, Scotland
Telephone: 44–4714– 216387

Southcornwall Yacht Charter

Cruising area: Ireland to Spain
Types of charters: Bareboat, crewed
Boat length: 26 to 41 feet
Number of boats: 14
High season: July 10–August 24

Low season: April 3–May 1 and September 25–October 30
Mailing address: Mylor Yacht Harbor, Falmouth, Cornwall TR11
  6UF, England
Telephone: 44–326–374204
Fax: 44–326–211591

Swan Sail Yacht Charter Ltd.

Cruising area: France, Corsica, Balearic Islands, Greece, Turkey,
  Canary Islands, Antilles
Types of charters: Bareboat, crewed
Boat length: 27 to 51 feet
Number of boats: Varies by location
High season: Varies by location
Low season: Varies by location
Mailing address: P.O. Box 77, Bury Lancs BL9 7YE, England
Telephone: 44–61–705228
Fax: 44–61–7972518

Templecraft Yacht Charters

Cruising area: France, Spain, Italy, Sardinia, Greece, Turkey
Types of charters: Bareboat, flotilla
Boat length: 28 to 51 feet
Number of boats: 120
High season: July 16–September 20
Low season: April 1–July 15 and September 21–October 31
Mailing address: 33 Grande Parade, Brighton BN2 2QA, England
Telephone: 44–273–695094
Fax: 44–273–688855

Ulster Cruising School

Cruising area: Irish Sea
Types of charters: Bareboat, crewed, sailing school
Boat length: 32 feet
Number of boats: 2
High season: June 1–August 30
Low season: March 1–April 30 and September 1–October 30
Mailing address: Marina Carrickfergus, County Antrim BT38
  8BE, Northern Ireland
Telephone: 44–9603–68818

Ulysses Yacht Charters
Cruising area: Ireland
Types of charters: Bareboat, crewed
Boat length: 26 to 34 feet
Number of boats: 4
High season: May 1–September 30
Low season: October 1–April 30
Mailing address: Bellmount House, Ballinea, Mullingar,
   Westmeath, Ireland
Telephone: 353–44–43558

Yacht Connections Ltd.
Cruising area: Virgin Islands, Leeward and Windward Islands,
   France, Italy, Balearic Islands, Yugoslavia, Greece, Turkey,
   Seychelles, Thailand
Types of charters: Crewed
Boat length: 40 to 75 feet
Number of boats: 100
High season: December 1–May 1
Low season: May 2–November 30
Mailing address: The Hames, 13 Church Road, South Ascot,
   Berkshire SL5 9DP, England
Telephone: 44–344–24987
Fax: 44–344–26849

Yachting International
Cruising area: Ireland
Types of charters: Bareboat, crewed
Boat length: 31 to 41 feet
Number of boats: 14
High season: June 1–August 30
Low season: March 1–May 31 and September 1–October 31
Mailing address: Trident Hotel, Kinsale, County Cork, Ireland
Telephone: Not available
Fax: 353–21–772927

Yachting Plus
Cruising area: Cote d'Azur, French Riviera, Corsica, Sardinia,
   Balearic Islands

Types of charters: Bareboat, crewed
Boat length: 26 to 42 feet
Number of boats: 25
High season: April 18–September 11
Low season: September 12–April 17
Mailing address: 83310 Les Marines de Cogolin, France
Telephone: 33–94–43–45–94
Fax: 33–94–43–47–85

Zeilwaart Enkhuizen
Cruising area: Netherlands, Brittany, Southern England, the
   Baltic (Denmark to Germany, and Sweden to Finland)
Types of charters: Bareboat, crewed
Boat length: Not available
Number of boats: 60
High season: April 1–September 30
Low season: Not available
Mailing address: Stationsplein 3, 1601 EN Enkhuizen, Holland
Telephone: 31–2280–12424
Fax: 31–2280–13737

Scandinavia

Lofoten Charter Boats:
Cruising area: Norway
Types of charters: Bareboat
Boat length: 29 to 95 feet
Number of boats: 15
High season: June 30–August 24
Low season: May 26–June 29 and January 3+May 25
Mailing address: Orneveien 1, 8550 Lodingin, Norway
Telephone: 47–82–31113
Fax: 47–82–32002

Norway Yacht Charter AC
Cruising area: Norway
Types of charters: Crewed
Boat length: 65 to 99 feet
Number of boats: 7
High season: May 1–August 30
Low season: April 1–April 30 and September 1–September 30
Mailing address: P.B. 91 Sentrum, 0101 Oslo, Norway
Telephone: 47–2–426498
Fax: 47–2–332346

Saimaa Sailing Oy
Cruising area: Finland
Types of charters: Bareboat
Boat length: 27 to 38 feet
Number of boats: 10
High season and low season: Not available
Mailing address: Kimpisenkatu, 22 53100 Lappeenranta, Finland
Telephone: 358–53–18560
Fax: 358–53–560640

Seil As
Cruising area: Norway
Types of charters: Bareboat

Boat length: 36 feet
Number of boats: 1
High season: June 1–August 30
Low season: May 1–May 31 and September 1–September 30
Mailing address: P.O. Box 156, 5046 Raadal, Norway
Telephone: 47–5–123536

Stavanger Yacht Charter
Cruising area: Norway
Types of charters: Bareboat, crewed
Boat length: 34 to 39 feet
Number of boats: 14
High season: June 15–August 15
Low season: May 1–June 14 and August 16–October 1
Mailing address: Tjeldveien 37, 4300 Sandnes, Norway
Telephone: 47–4–623191

Vuokra Venho
Cruising area: Finland
Types of charters: Not available
Boat length: Not available
Number of boats: Not available
High season: June 15–August 15
Low season: None
Mailing address: Olaviwkatu 26 57230, Savonlinna, Finland
Telephone: 358–49–673055
Fax: 358–57–13101

West Marine International A/S Ltd.
Cruising area: Norway
Types of charters: Bareboat
Boat length: 36 to 42 feet
Number of boats: 2
High season: June 1–August 15
Low season: April 1–May 31 and August 16–October 15
Mailing address: Skuteviksboder 19, 5035 Bergen, Norway
Telephone: 47–5–312525

Zeilwaart Enkhuizen

Cruising area: Netherlands, Brittany, Southern England, the
  Baltic (Denmark to Germany, and Sweden to Finland)
Types of charters: Bareboat, crewed
Boat length: Not available
Number of boats: 60
High season: April 1–September 30
Low season: Not available
Mailing address: Stationsplein 3, 1601 EN Enkhuizen, Holland
Telephone: 31–2280–12424
Fax: 31–2280–13737

The Mediterranean

Aegean Yacht Services
Cruising area: Greece, Turkey
Types of charters: Bareboat, crewed
Boat length: 27 to 83 feet
Number of boats: 21
High season: July 1–August 30
Low season: May 1–June 30 and September 1–October 30
Mailing address: P.O. Box 155 Bodrum, Turkey
Telephone: 90–6141–1734

Albatross P.Y.C.C.
Cruising area: Greece, Turkey
Types of charters: Bareboat, crewed, flotilla
Boat length: 31 to 51 feet
Number of boats: 100-plus
High season: April 25–October 10
Low season: October 11–April 24
Mailing address: 56 Merrice Avenue, Merrick, NY 11566
Telephone: (800) 922–4864 or (516) 867–1957

Apollonia Yachts Ltd.
Cruising area: Greece, Turkey
Types of charters: Bareboat, crewed
Boat length: 29 to 78 feet
Number of boats: 38
High season: July 25–August 29
Low season: April 25–July 24 and August 30–October 10
Mailing address: 1, Makariou St., Kalamaki, Athens 174 55,
   Greece
Telephone: 30–98–23–901
Fax: 30–93–81–103

A.T.C. Group
Cruising area: Turkey
Types of charters: Crewed

Boat length: 38 to 72 feet
Number of boats: 10
High season: July 1–September 30
Low season: April 1–June 30 and October 1–November 30
Mailing address: P.O. Box 166, Marmaris 48700, Turkey
Telephone: 90–612–13835
Fax: 90–612–16550

ATM Yachts

Cruising area: Caribbean (St. Martin, Guadeloupe, Martinique, Leeward Islands, Pacific (French Polynesia), Mediterranean (Marseilles)
Types of charters: Bareboat, crewed (flotilla in Martinique only)
Boat length: 36 to 55 feet
Number of boats: Varies by location from 12 to 200
High season: Caribbean, December 20–May 3; French Polynesia, July 1–August 31; Mediterranean, not available
Low season: Caribbean, May 4–December 19; French Polynesia, September 1–June 30; Mediterranean, not available
Mailing address: 2280 University Drive, Suite 102, Newport Beach, CA 92660
Telephone: (800) 634–8822 or (714) 650–0889
Fax: (714) 642–1318

ARGO Yachting

Cruising area: Greece, Turkey
Types of charters: Bareboat, crewed, flotilla
Boat length: 31 to 57 feet
Number of boats: 170
High season: July 25–August 30
Low season: April 25–July 24 and September 1–October 10
Mailing address: 8, Athan, Daikou Str., 142 33 N. Ionia, Athens, Greece
Telephone: 30–27–98–423
Fax: 30–27–51–589

Buoys Cruising Club

Cruising area: Greece
Types of charters: Bareboat, crewed

The road up to the town of Spartahori, Greek Islands

Boat length: 32 to 45 feet
Number of boats: 5
High season: July 1–August 30
Low season: March 15–June 30 and September 1–October 30
Mailing address: 8 Chase Side, Enfield, Middlesex EN2 6NF,
   England
Telephone: 44–81–367–8462
Fax: 44–81–367–8462

Carefree Sailing Ltd.
Cruising area: Greece
Types of charters: Bareboat, crewed
Boat length: 31 to 55 feet
Number of boats: Not available
High season: July 25–August 29
Low season: October 13–April 23
Mailing address: 111 Aretis St., Ano Glyfada, 16674, Athens,
   Greece
Telephone: 30–1–962–5216

Charter Plus
Cruising area: French Mediterranean
Types of charters: Bareboat, flotilla
Boat length: 25 to 39 feet
Number of boats: 5
High season: July 1–August 30
Low season: March 1–June 30 and September 1–November 30
Mailing address: 2 Victoria Road, Mudeford, Christchurch,
   Dorset BH23 3LF, England
Telephone: 44–202–478248

Club Voyages
Cruising area: Turkey, Greece, Yugoslavia
Types of charters: Bareboat, crewed, flotilla
Boat length: 30 to 57 feet
Number of boats: 25
High season: May 1–September 30
Low season: April 1–April 30 and October 1–October 31
Mailing address: Box 7648, Shrewsbury, NJ 07702

Telephone: (908) 291–8228
Fax: (908) 291–4277

Enterprise Sailing
Cruising area: Balearic Islands, Italy, Sardinia, Greece, Turkey,
  British Virgin Islands
Types of charters: Bareboat, crewed
Boat length: 28 to 45 feet
Number of boats: 80
High season: July 1–September 1
Low season: September 2–June 30
Mailing address: 36 Hart Street, Henvey-On-Thames, Oxon
  RG9 2AU, England
Telephone: 44–491–410411

First Class Yachting AB
Cruising area: Turkey
Types of charters: Bareboat, crewed
Boat length: 35 to 51 feet
Number of boats: 28
High season: May 1–September 30
Low season: April 1–April 30 and October 1–November 30
Mailing address: Karl X Gustavs gata 58, S-254 40 Helsingborg,
  Sweden
Telephone: 46–10–4642–128781

GM Yachting Enterprises Ltd.
Cruising area: Greece
Types of charters: Bareboat, crewed
Boat length: 26 to 105 feet
Number of boats: 80
High season: July 24–August 21
Low season: April 25–July 24 and August 22–October 10
Mailing address: Markariou Str. 2, GR 174 55, Kalamaki,
  Athens, Greece
Telephone: 30–01–9815–619

Golden Pheasant Yacht Charter
Cruising area: Greece, Turkey, Venezuela

Types of charters: Crewed
Boat length: 50 feet
Number of boats: 1
High season: June 1–August 30
Low season: September 1–May 31
Mailing address: 20 Phillimore Gardens, London W8 6S9, England
Telephone: 44–71–937–4445

GPSC Charters Ltd.

Cruising area: Greece, Turkey
Types of charters: Bareboat, crewed, flotilla
Boat length: 40 to 56 feet
Number of boats: 12
High season: May 1–September 30
Low season: April 1–April 30 and October 1–October 31
Mailing address: 600 St. Andrew Road, Philadelphia, PA 19118
Telephone: (800) 732–6786 or (215) 247–3903
Fax: (215) 247–1505

Kalymna Yachting Ltd.

Cruising area: Greece, Turkey
Types of charters: Bareboat, crewed
Boat length: 30 to 48 feet
Number of boats: 20
High season: July 25–August 29
Low season: March 28–May 1 and October 4–November 14
Mailing address: P.O. Box 47, 85200 Kalymnos, Greece
Telephone: 30–243–24083
Fax: 29125

McCulloch Yacht Charter

Cruising area: Greece, Turkey
Types of charters: Crewed
Boat length: 37 to 159 feet
Number of boats: 20-plus
High season: July 1–September 15
Low season: May 1–June 30 and September 16–October 15
Mailing address: 60 Fordwych Road, London NW2 3TH, England
Telephone and fax: 44–81–452–7509

The Moorings
Cruising area: British Virgin Islands, Bahamas, Martinique to Grenada, St. Martin, Guadeloupe, Sea of Cortez, Tahiti, Tonga, Thailand, Greece, Turkey, Yugoslavia, Corsica, Brittany, Spain, Italy, France
Types of charters: Bareboat, crewed, flotilla
Boat length: Varies by location (27 to 60 feet)
Number of boats: Varies by location (600-plus)
High season: Varies by location
Low season: Varies by location
Mailing address: 19345 U.S. 19 North, Clearwater, FL 34624
Telephone: (800) 535–7289 or (813) 530–5424
Fax: (813) 530–9747

Nava Yachts
Cruising area: Greece
Types of charters: Bareboat, crewed
Boat length: 42 feet
Number of boats: 20
High season: April 24–October 9
Low season: October 10–April 23
Mailing address: 6 Loudovikou Square, Piraeus, Greece
Telephone: 30–1–417–7728

Naviera Formentor SA
Cruising area: Balearic Islands
Types of charters: Bareboat, crewed, flotilla
Boat length: 35 to 65 feet
Number of boats: 7
High season: April 25–October 9
Low season: April 1–April 24 and October 10–October 30
Mailing address: Jardines de S. Telmo s/n, 07012 Palma de Mallorca
Telephone: 71–71–09–49
Fax: 71–71–95–98

Odysseus Yachting Holidays
Cruising area: Greece
Types of charters: Bareboat, flotilla

Boat length: 29 to 40 feet
Number of boats: 40
High season: July 11–July 31
Low season: August 1–July 10
Mailing address: 33 Grande Parade, Brighton BN2 2QA, England
Telephone: 44–273–695094

Osprey Cruising Ltd.
Cruising area: Greece, Turkey
Types of charters: Crewed
Boat length: 79 feet
Number of boats: 5
High season: July 1–August 30
Low season: May 1–June 30 and September 1–October 31
Mailing address: Royal Oak Inn, Laxfield, Woodbridge, Suffolk
   1P13 8DH, England
Telephone: 44–986–798446

Paul Vasilakis
Cruising area: Greece
Types of charters: Bareboat
Boat length: 34 feet
Number of boats: 1
High season: June 16–August 30
Low season: September 1–May 31
Mailing address: 157 Aristdoy Str., 176-72 Kallithea, Athens,
   Greece
Telephone: 30–1–9597–331
Fax: 30–1–8940–840

Pellele Cruises Ltd.
Cruising area: Greece, Turkey
Types of charters: Crewed
Boat length: 70 feet
Number of boats: 1
High season: Not available
Low season: Not available
Mailing address: P.O. Box 4875, Nicosia, Cyprus
Telephone: 357–2–314547

Seaquest Holidays

Cruising area: Turkey
Types of charters: Bareboat, crewed
Boat length: 33 to 44 feet
Number of boats: 6
High season: May 1–September 30
Low season: April 1–April 30 and October 1–October 31
Mailing address: 9 Grand Parade, Green Lanes, Haringey,
  London N4 15X, England
Telephone: 44–81–800–8030

Sovereign Sailing

Cruising area: Sardinia, Greece, Turkey
Types of charters: Bareboat, flotilla
Boat length: 27 to 34 feet
Number of boats: 85
High season: July 1–August 30
Low season: Not available
Mailing address: 390 London Road, Crawley, West Sussex RH10
  2TB, England
Telephone: 44–293–599944

Stelmaros Sailing Ltd.

Cruising area: Greece
Types of charters: Bareboat
Boat length: 31 feet
Number of boats: 1
High season: July 1–August 30
Low season: April 1–June 30 and September 1–October 30
Mailing address: 31, Withnell Fold, NR Chorley, Lanes PR6
  8BA, England
Telephone: 44–254–830390

Sunsail

Cruising area: Bahamas, British and U.S. Virgin Islands, St.
  Martin, Anguilla, St. Barts, Antigua, Martinique to Grenada,
  Corsica, Sardinia, Greece, Turkey, Yugoslavia, Thailand
Types of charters: Bareboat, crewed, flotilla
Boat length: 29 to 56 feet

Number of boats: Varies by location (7 to 50)
High season and low season: Varies by location
Mailing address: 2 Prospect Park, 3347 NW Fifty-fifth Street,
 Fort Lauderdale, FL 33309
Telephone: (800) 327–2276

Swan Sail Yacht Charter Ltd.

Cruising area: France, Corsica, Balearic Islands, Greece, Turkey,
 Canary Islands, Antilles
Types of charters: Bareboat, crewed
Boat length: 27 to 51 feet
Number of boats: Varies by location
High season and low season: Varies by location
Mailing address: P.O. Box 77, Bury Lancs. BL9 7YE, England
Telephone: 44–61–705228
Fax: 44–61–7972518

Templecraft Yacht Charters

Cruising area: France, Spain, Italy, Sardinia, Greece, Turkey
Types of charters: Bareboat, flotilla
Boat length: 28 to 51 feet
Number of boats: 120
High season: July 16–September 20
Low season: April 1–July 15 and September 21–October 31
Mailing address: 33 Grand Parade, Brighton BN2 2QA, England
Telephone: 44–273–695094
Fax: 44–273–688855

Tenrag Yacht Charters

Cruising area: Greece, Turkey, Malaysia
Types of charters: Bareboat, crewed, flotilla
Boat length: 28 to 68 feet
Number of boats: 30
High season: July 1–August 30
Low season: Not available
Mailing address: Bramling House, Bramling, Canterbury, Kent
 CT3 1NB, England
Telephone: 44–227–721874 or 44–227–721875
Fax: 44–227–721684

Top Yacht Charter Ltd.
Cruising area: Greece, Turkey
Types of charters: Bareboat, crewed
Boat length: 30 to 49 feet
Number of boats: 22
High season: Not available
Low season: Not available
Mailing address: Andrew Hill Lane, Hedgerley, Bucks SL2 3UW, England
Telephone: 44–753–646636

Valef Yachts Ltd.
Cruising area: Greece, Turkey
Types of charters: Bareboat, crewed
Boat length: 46 to 140 feet
Number of boats: 300-plus
High season: March 1–October 31
Low season: None
Mailing address: P.O. Box 391, Ambler, PA 19002
Telephone: (800) 223–3845

Yacht Connections Ltd.
Cruising area: Virgin Islands, Leeward and Windward Islands, France, Italy, Balearic Islands, Yugoslavia, Greece, Turkey, Seychelles, Thailand
Types of charters: Crewed
Boat length: 40 to 75 feet
Number of boats: 100
High season: December 1–May 1
Low season: May 2–November 30
Mailing address: The Hames, 13 Church Road, South Ascot, Berkshire SL5 9DP, England
Telephone: 44–344–24987
Fax: 44–344–26849

Yachting Plus
Cruising area: Cote d'Azur, French Riviera, Corsica, Sardinia, Balearic Islands
Types of charters: Bareboat, crewed

Boat length: 26 to 42 feet
Number of boats: 25
High season: April 18–September 11
Low season: September 12–April 17
Mailing address: 83310 Les Marines de Cogolin, France
Telephone: 33–94–43–45–94
Fax: 33–94–43–47–85

Yuksel Yachting
Cruising area: Turkey
Types of charters: Bareboat
Boat length: 33 to 51 feet
Number of boats: Not available
High season: April 28–September 28
Low season: April 1–April 27 and September 29–November 30
Mailing address: Barbados Caddesi 263, P.O. Box 126,
   Marmaris, Turkey
Telephone: 90–6121–1016

Australia, New Zealand, Thailand, and the Seychelles

Apollo Charters
Cruising area: Whitsunday Islands, Australia
Types of charters: Bareboat, crewed, flotilla
Boat length: 37 to 54 feet
Number of boats: 3
High season and low season: Not available
Mailing address: P.O. Box 532, Airlie Beach, Queensland 4802, Australia
Telephone: 61–79–469334
Fax: 61–79–469532

Australian Bareboat Charters
Cruising area: Whitsunday Islands, Australia
Types of charters: Bareboat, crewed, flotilla
Boat length: 28 to 47 feet
Number of boats: 24
High season: September 19–January 15
Low season: January 16–September 18
Mailing address: P.O. Box 357, Airlie Beach, Queensland 4802, Australia
Telephone: 61–79–469381
Fax: 61–79–469220

Charter Link
Cruising area: Hauraki Gulf and Bay of Islands, New Zealand
Types of charters: Bareboat, crewed
Boat length: 28 to 36 feet
Number of boats: 15
High season: December 15–February 15
Low season: April 20–October 23
Mailing address: P.O. Box 82111, Highland Park, Auckland, New Zealand
Telephone: 64–9–5358710
Fax: 64–9–5730196

Coral Trekker Sailing Safaris

Cruising area: Whitsunday Islands and Great Barrier Reef, Australia
Types of charters: Crewed
Boat length: 75-foot square rigger
Number of boats: 1
High season: April 1–December 31
Low season: January 1–March 31
Mailing address: P.O. Box 519, Airlie Beach, Queensland 4802, Australia
Telephone: 61–79–467197
Fax: 61–79–467585

Cumberland Charter Yachts

Cruising area: Whitsunday Islands, Cumberland Group, Australia
Types of charters: Bareboat, crewed
Boat length: 28 to 38 feet
Number of boats: 17
High season and low season: Same
Mailing address: P.O. Box 49, Airlie Beach, Queensland 4802, Australia
Telephone: 61–8–075101 or 61–79–467500
Fax: 61–79–466230

Fame Yacht Charter

Cruising area: Great Barrier Reef and Whitsunday Islands, Australia
Types of charters: Crewed
Boat length: 40 to 74 feet
Number of boats: Not available
High season: Not available
Low season: Not available
Mailing address: RSD Victor Harbor, South Australia 5211
Telephone: 61–85–985321
Fax: 61–85–524478

Hamilton Island Charters

Cruising area: Whitsunday Islands, Australia
Types of charters: Bareboat, crewed

Boat length: 32 to 45 feet
Number of boats: Not available
High season: Not available
Low season: Not available
Mailing address: P.O. Box 35, Hamilton Island, Queensland
4803, Australia
Telephone: 61–79–469144
Fax: 61–79–469393

Mandalay Boat Charters

Cruising area: Whitsunday Islands, Australia
Types of charters: Bareboat, crewed
Boat length: 23 to 44 feet
Number of boats: 14
High season: Not available
Low season: Not available
Mailing address: P.O. Box 273, Airlie Beach, Queensland 4802,
Australia
Telephone: 61–79–466298
Fax: 61–79–466211

The Moorings

Cruising area: British Virgin Islands, Bahamas, Martinique to
Grenada, St. Martin, Guadeloupe, Sea of Cortez, Tahiti, Tonga,
Thailand, Greece, Turkey, Yugoslavia, Corsica, Brittany, Spain,
Italy, France
Types of charters: Bareboat, crewed, flotilla
Boat length: Varies by location (27 to 60 feet)
Number of boats: Varies by location (600-plus)
High season: Varies by location
Low season: Varies by location
Mailing address: 19345 U.S. 19 North, Clearwater, FL 34624
Telephone: (800) 535–7289 or (813) 530–5424
Fax: (813) 530–9747

Queensland Yacht Charters

Cruising area: Whitsunday and Cumberland islands, Australia
Types of charters: Bareboat, flotilla
Boat length: 30 to 72 feet

Number of boats: 17
High season: June 20–July 17, September 19–October 16,
   December 19–January 15, April 9–April 30
Low season: May 1–June 19, July 18–September 18, October
   17–December 18, January 16–April 8
Mailing address: P.O. Box 293, Airlie Beach, Queensland 4802,
   Australia
Telephone: 61–79–467400
Fax: 61–79–467698

South Seas Yacht Charters Ltd.
Cruising area: New Zealand
Types of charters: Bareboat, crewed, sailing school
Boat length: 20 to 35 feet
Number of boats: 8
High season: February 15–February 28
Low season: Not available
Mailing address: P.O. Box 38-366, Howick, Auckland, New
   Zealand
Telephone: 64–9–534–2001

Sunsail
Cruising area: Bahamas, British and U.S. Virgin Islands, St.
   Martin, Anguilla, St. Barts, Antigua, Martinique to Grenada,
   Corsica, Sardinia, Greece, Turkey, Yugoslavia
Types of charters: Bareboat, crewed, flotilla
Boat length: 29 to 56 feet
Number of boats: Varies by location (7 to 50)
High season: Varies by location
Low season: Varies by location
Mailing address: 2 Prospect Park, 3347 NW Fifty-fifth Street,
   Fort Lauderdale, FL 33309
Telephone: (800) 327–2276

Tenrag Yacht Charters
Cruising area: Greece, Turkey, Malaysia
Types of charters: Bareboat, crewed, flotilla
Boat length: 28 to 68 feet
Number of boats: 30

High season: July 1–August 30
Low season: Not available
Mailing address: Bramling House, Bramling, Canterbury, Kent CT3 1NB, England
Telephone: 44–227–721874 or 44–227–721875
Fax: 44–227–721684

Whitsunday Rent A Yacht
Cruising area: Whitsunday Islands, Australia
Types of charters: Bareboat, crewed
Boat length: 27 to 43 feet
Number of boats: 35
High season: Not available
Low season: Not available
Mailing address: PMB 25 Mackay, Queensland 4741, Australia
Telephone: 61–79–469232
Fax: 61–79–469512

Yacht Connections Ltd.
Cruising area: Virgin Islands, Leeward and Windward Islands, France, Italy, Balearic Islands, Yugoslavia, Greece, Turkey, Seychelles, Thailand
Types of charters: Crewed
Boat length: 40 to 75 feet
Number of boats: 100
High season: December 1–May 1
Low season: May 2–November 30
Mailing address: The Hames, 13 Church Road, South Ascot, Berkshire SL5 9DP, England
Telephone: 44–344–24987
Fax: 44–344– 26849

The Pacific

ATM Yachts
Cruising area: Caribbean (St. Martin, Guadeloupe, Martinique, Leeward Islands, Pacific (French Polynesia), Mediterranean (Marseilles)
Types of charters: Bareboat, crewed (flotilla in Martinique only)
Boat length: 36 to 55 feet
Number of boats: Varies by location from 12 to 200
High season: Caribbean, December 20–May 3; French Polynesia, July 1–August 31; Mediterranean, not available
Low season: Caribbean, May 4–December 19; French Polynesia, September 1–June 30; Mediterranean, not available
Mailing address: 2280 University Drive, Suite 102, Newport Beach, CA 92660
Telephone: (800) 634–8822 or (714) 650–0889
Fax: (714) 642–1318

Captain Andy's Sailing Adventures
Cruising area: Hawaii
Types of charters: Bareboat, crewed
Boat length: 46 feet
Number of boats: 2
High season: Not available
Low season: Not available
Mailing address: P.O. Box 1291, Koloa, HI 96756
Telephone: (808) 822–7833

Emerald Yacht Charters Ltd.
Cruising area: Fiji
Types of charters: Crewed
Boat length: 35 to 43 feet
Number of boats: 3
High season: Not available
Low season: Not available
Mailing address: P.O. Box 15, Savusavu, Fiji
Telephone: 679–850–440

Hawaii Bluewater Sailing

Cruising area: Hawaii
Types of charters: Crewed
Boat length: 36 & 38 feet
Number of boats: 2
High season: Not available
Low season: Not available
Mailing address: P.O. Box 1813, Honakaa, HI 96727
Telephone: (808) 326–1986

Honolulu Sailing Company

Cruising area: Hawaii
Types of charters: Bareboat, crewed, flotilla
Boat length: 36 to 71 feet
Number of boats: 6
High season: Not available
Low season: Not available
Mailing address: 47-335 Lulani Street, Kaneoha, HI 96744
Telephone: (808) 239–3900 or (808) 829–0114
Fax: (808) 236–0008

Maile

Cruising area: Hawaii
Types of charters: Crewed
Boat length: 50 feet
Number of boats: 1
High season: November 1–February 28
Low season: Not available
Mailing address: P.O. Box 44335, Kamuela, HI 96743
Telephone: (808) 885–6514

The Moorings

Cruising area: British Virgin Islands, Bahamas, Martinique to
    Grenada, St. Martin, Guadeloupe, Sea of Cortez, Tahiti, Tonga,
    Thailand, Greece, Turkey, Yugoslavia, Corsica, Brittany, Spain,
    Italy, France
Types of charters: Bareboat, crewed, flotilla
Boat length: Varies by location (27 to 60 feet)
Number of boats: Varies by location (600-plus)

High season: Varies by location
Low season: Varies by location
Mailing address: 19345 U.S. 19 North, Clearwater, FL 34624
Telephone: (800) 535–7289 or (813) 530–5424
Fax: (813) 530–9747

Rainbow Yacht Charters
Cruising area: New Zealand, Vava'u Islands, Tonga
Types of charters: Bareboat, crewed, flotilla, sailing school
Boat length: 35 to 43 feet
Number of boats: 40
High season: Tonga—year-round; New Zealand—December
   21–February 28
Low season: New Zealand—March 1–December 20
Mailing address: P.O. Box 8327, Symonds Street, Auckland,
   New Zealand
Telephone: 64–9–3780–719
Fax: 64–9–3780–931

Rose Marine, Inc.
Cruising area: Hawaii
Types of charters: Crewed
Boat length: 36 to 50 feet
Number of boats: 4
High season: Not available
Low season: Not available
Mailing address: P.O. Box 831, Lahaina Harbor, Lahaina, HI 96767
Telephone: (808) 667–9089

Trimarine Boat Co. Ltd.
Cruising area: British Virgin Islands, Galapagos Islands
Types of charters: Crewed
Boat length: 95 and 105 feet
Number of boats: 2
High season: Not available
Low season: Not available
Mailing address: P.O. Box 362, Road Town, Tortola, BVI
Telephone: (809) 494–2490
Fax: (809) 494–5774

Tumbaco, Inc.
Cruising area: Galapagos Islands
Types of charters: Crewed
Boat length: 56 to 93 feet
Number of boats: 3
High season: Year-round
Low season: None
Mailing address: P.O. Box 1036, Punta Gorda, FL 33951
Telephone: (800) 247–2925 or (813) 637–4660
Fax: (813) 637–9876

Index

About the Authors

Melvin H. Ross has been an avid sailor for twenty-nine years and is a frequent contributor to sailing publications. Many of his articles describe his adventures sailing chartered boats in exotic locales. He has chartered throughout the Caribbean, the Mediterranean, and the Orient, most recently off the coast of Thailand. Ross served as Commodore of the Senasqua Boating Association and has been an active member of the Yacht Cruising Association and BOAT U.S. for many years.

James P. Duffy is a weekend sailor and professional writer. His seven previously published books include *How to Go Bankrupt Without Going Broke* (Pharos, 1992), *Learn While You Sleep* (Avon, 1991), *Cutting College Costs* (Harper & Row, 1988), and *Family First Aid* (Harris, 1979).

Outdoor Recreation

Here are some other fine titles on a host of outdoor recreation activities, from sea kayaking to hiking the wilderness. All Globe Pequot outdoor recreation titles are written by experts in the field and will help you to find hours of outdoor enjoyment. Please check your local bookstore for other fine Globe Pequot Press titles, which include:

Striper Surf, $22.95
Seekers of the Horizon, $22.95 HC
The Coastal Kayaker, $12.95
The Coastal Kayaker's Manual, $12.95
Derek C. Hutchinson's Guide to Sea Kayaking, $13.95
Fundamentals of Kayak Navigation, $14.95
Reading the Water, $13.95
National Parks Fishing Guide, $16.95
Whitewater Rafting in Eastern North America, $11.95
Whitewater Rafting in Western North America, $13.95
Guide to National Park Areas: East, $14.95
Guide to National Park Areas: West, $14.95
Canoeing Made Easy, $14.95

To order any of these titles with MasterCard or Visa, call toll-free (800) 243–0495; in Connecticut call (800) 962–0973. Free shipping for orders of three or more books. Shipping charge of $3.00 per book for one or two books ordered. Connecticut residents add sales tax. Ask for your free catalogue of Globe Pequot's quality books on recreation, travel, nature, gardening, cooking, crafts, and more. Prices and availability subject to change.